I0698372

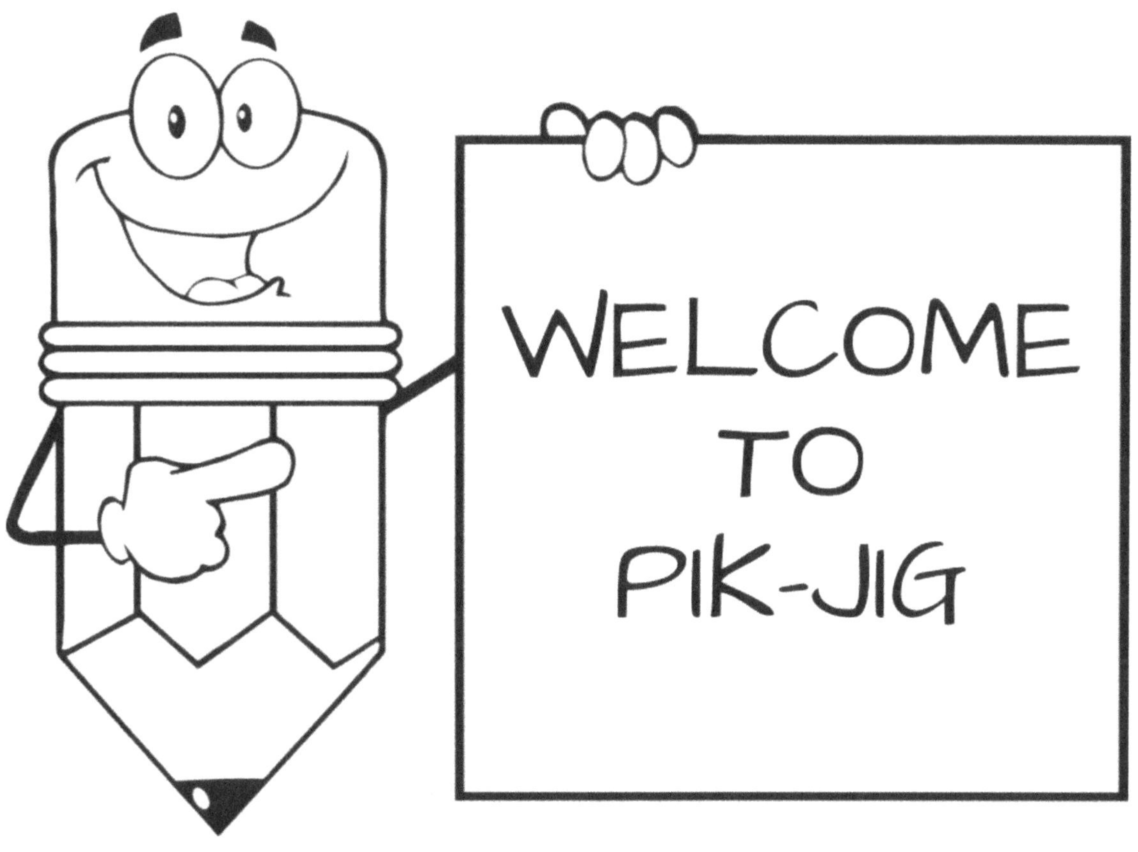

WELCOME
TO
PIK-JIG

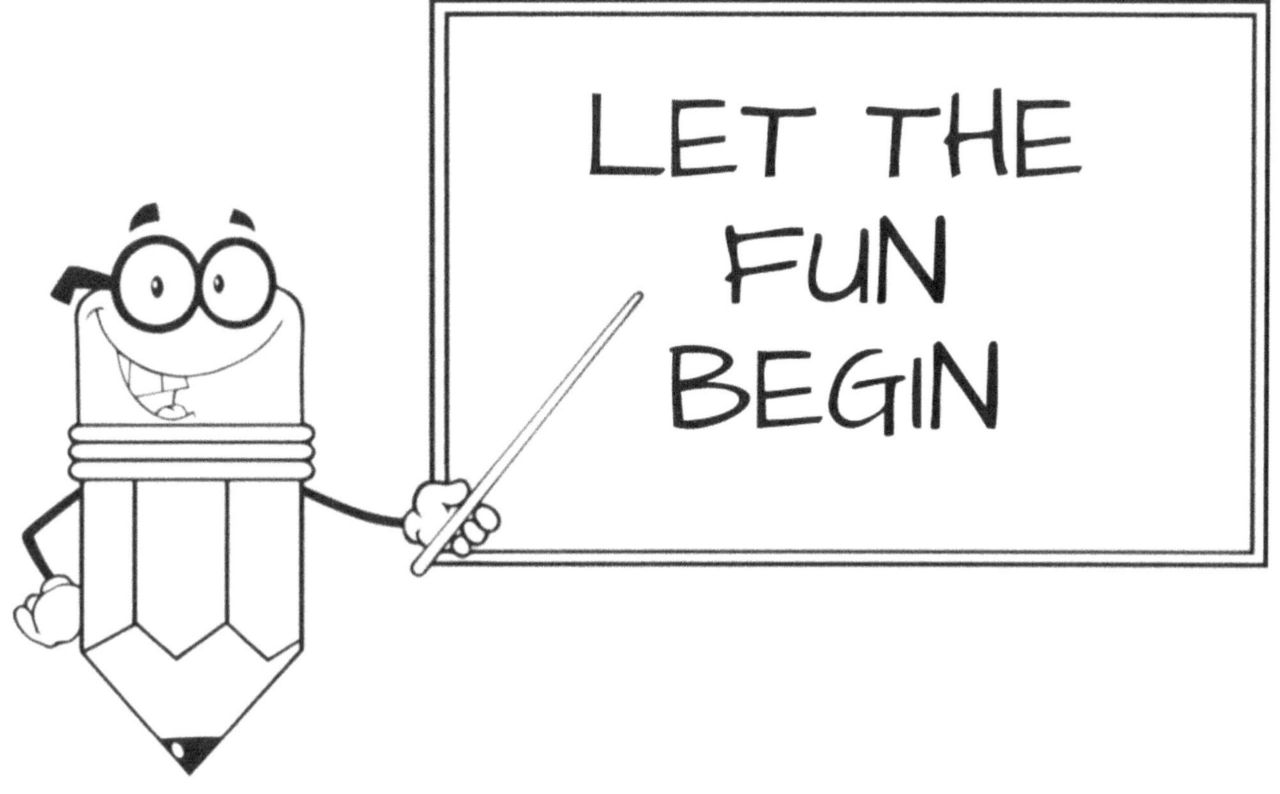

Copyright © 2024 by Pik-Jig

All rights reserved.

INSTRUCTIONS

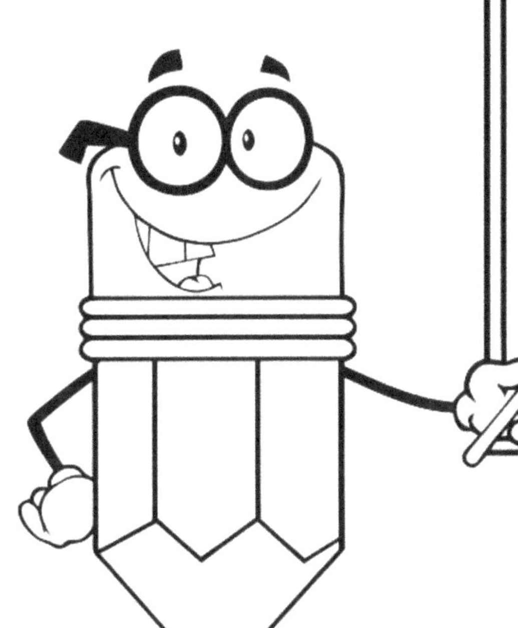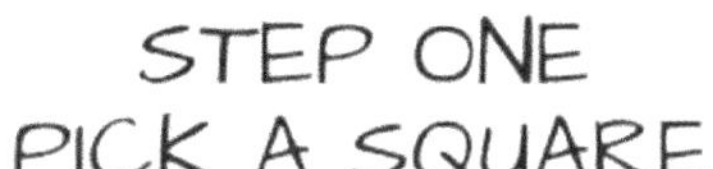

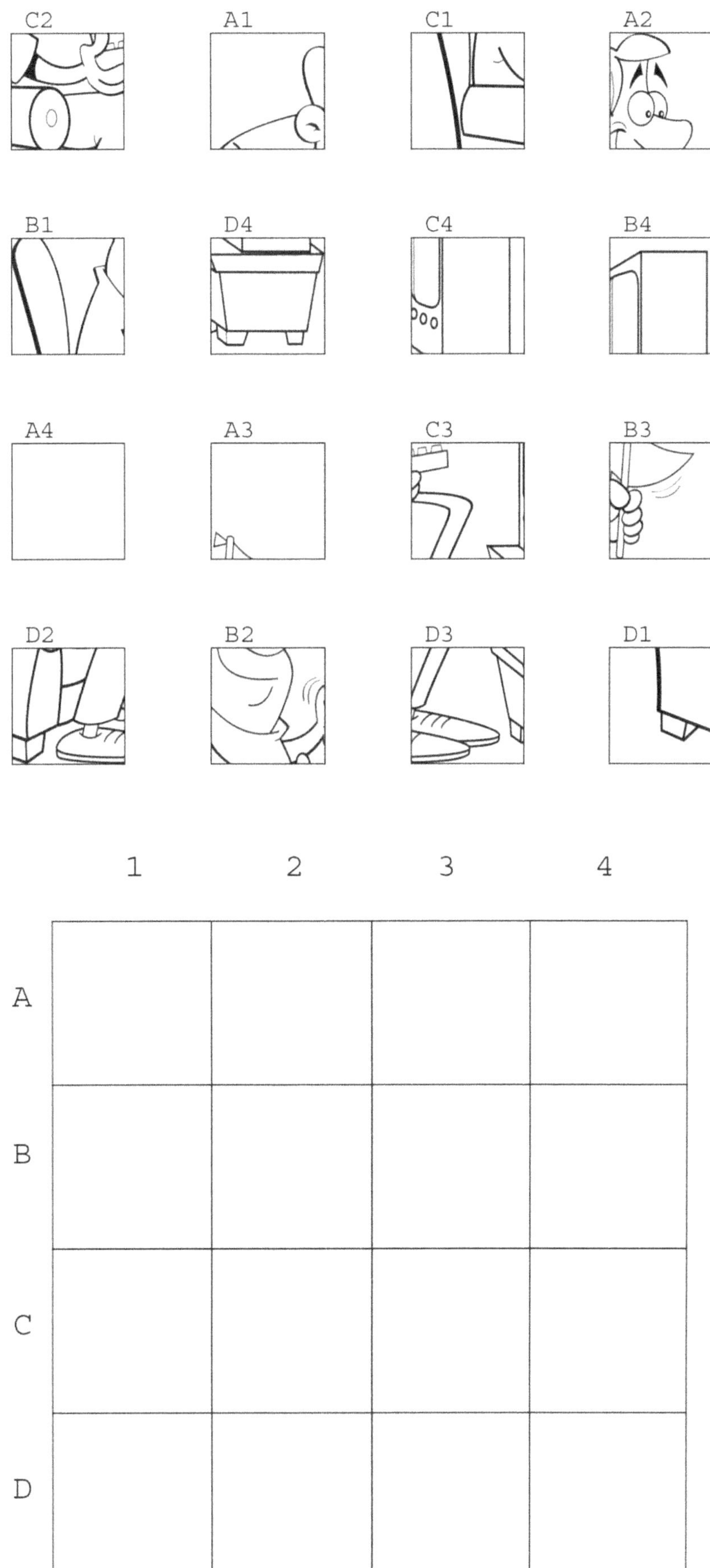

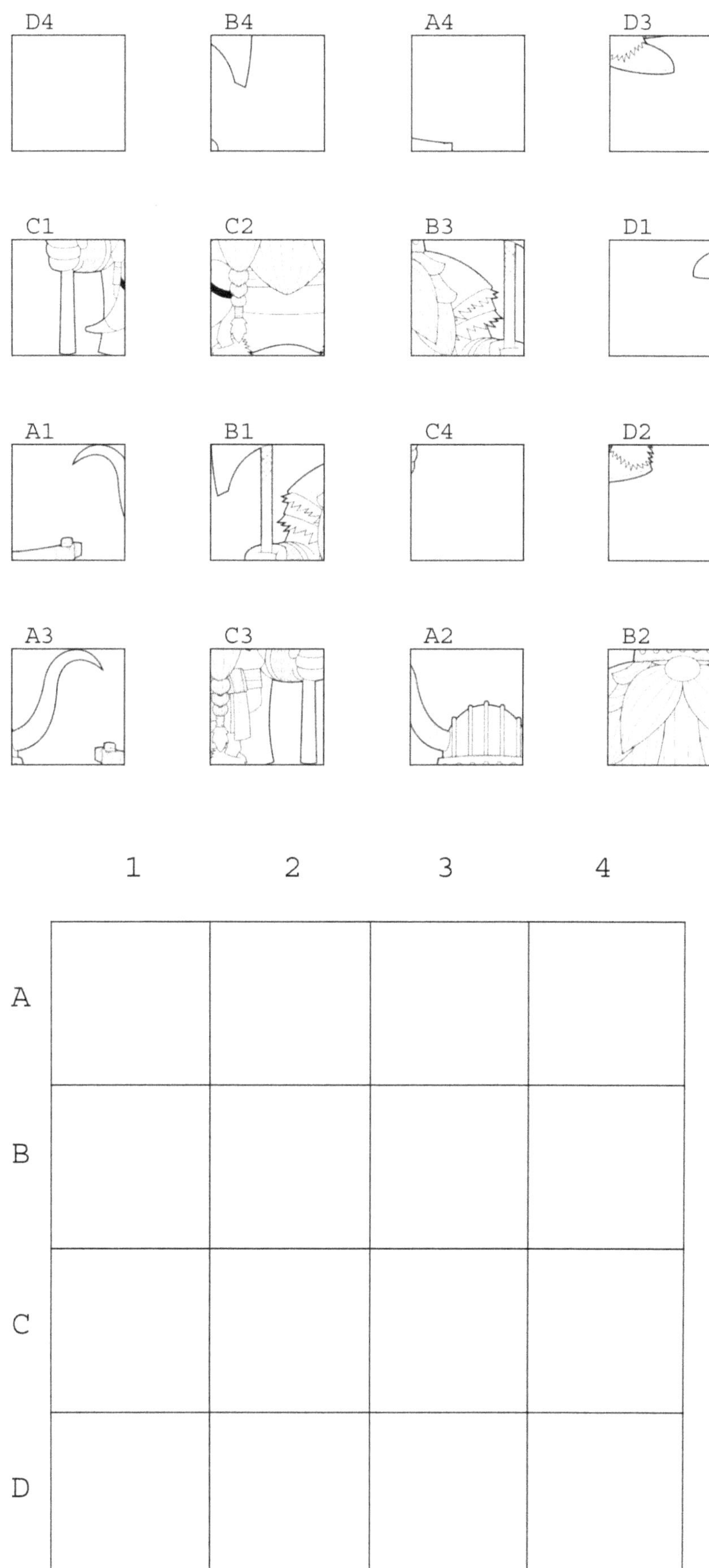

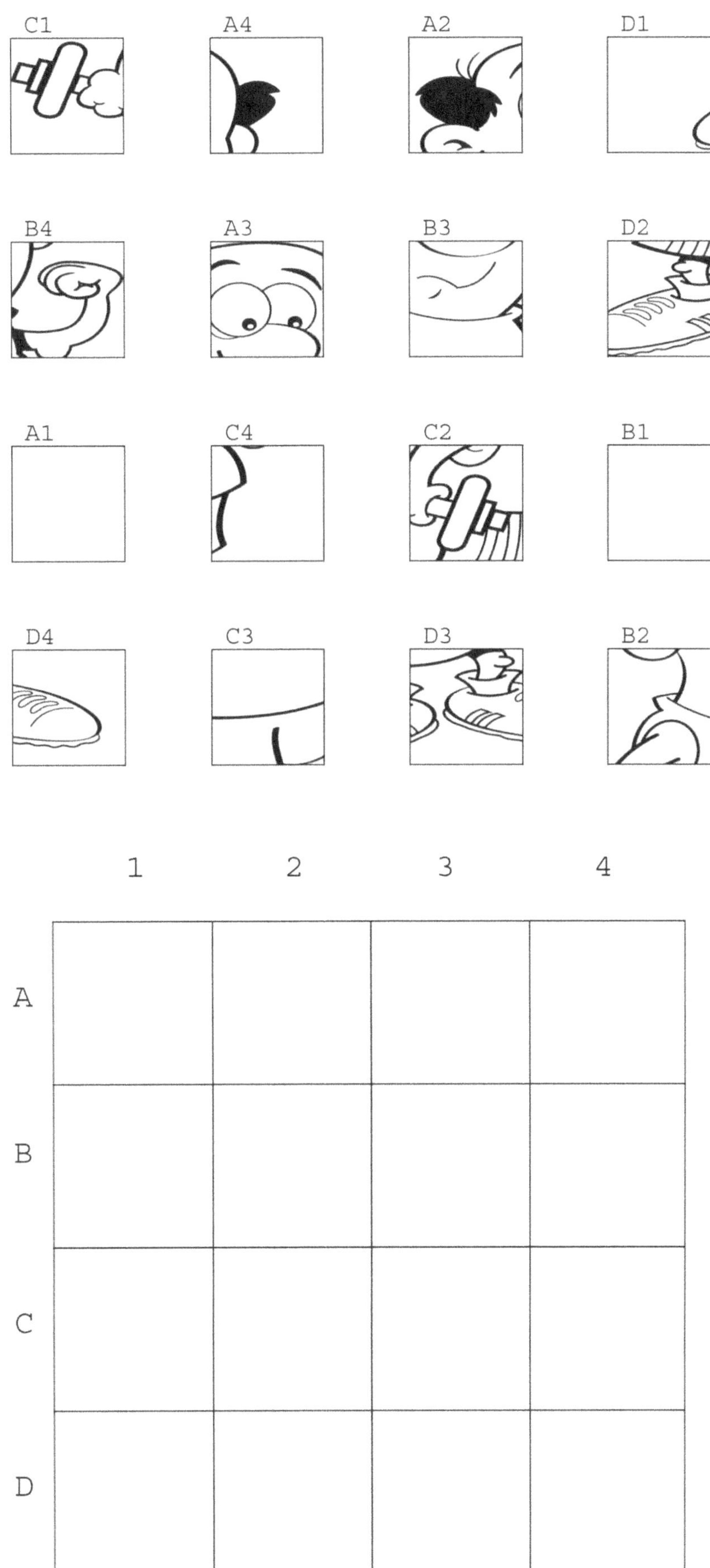

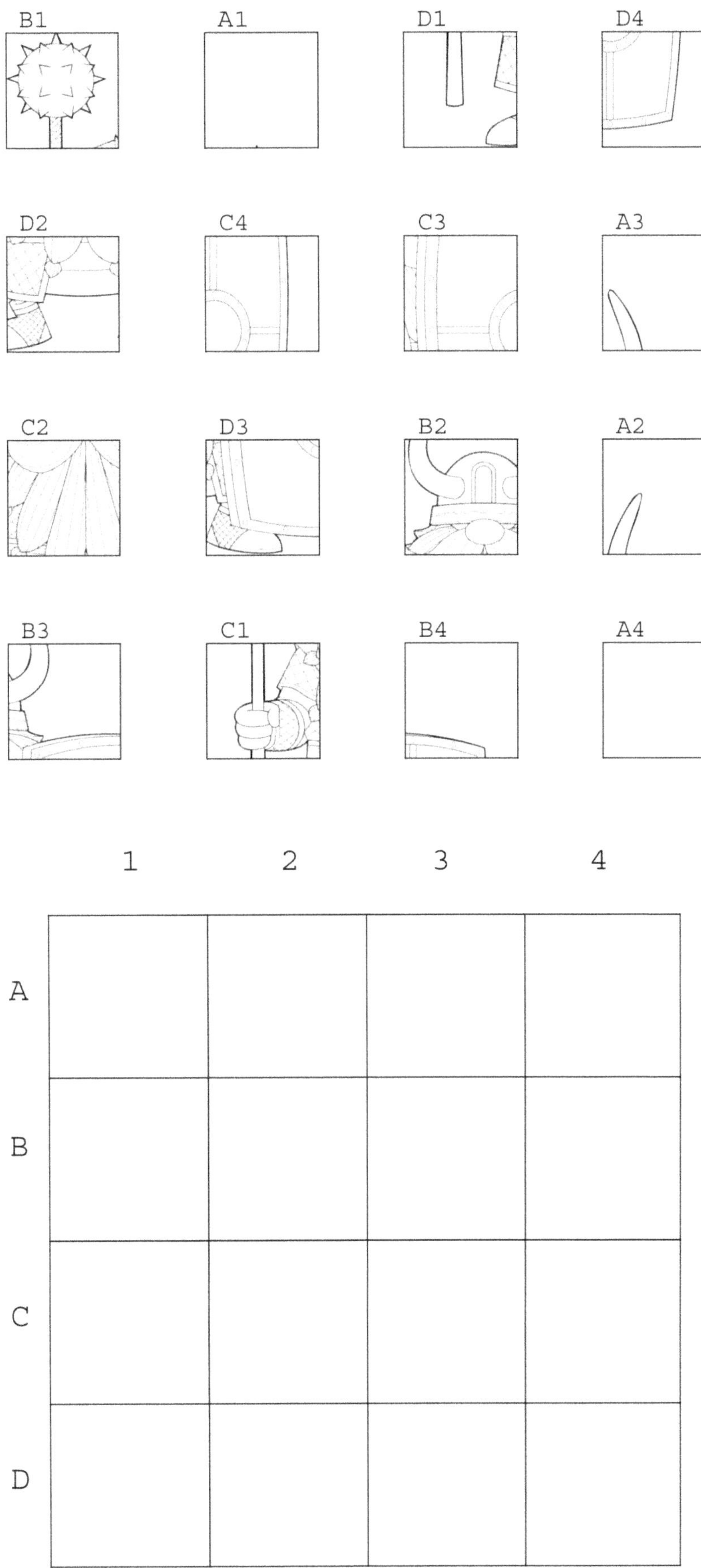

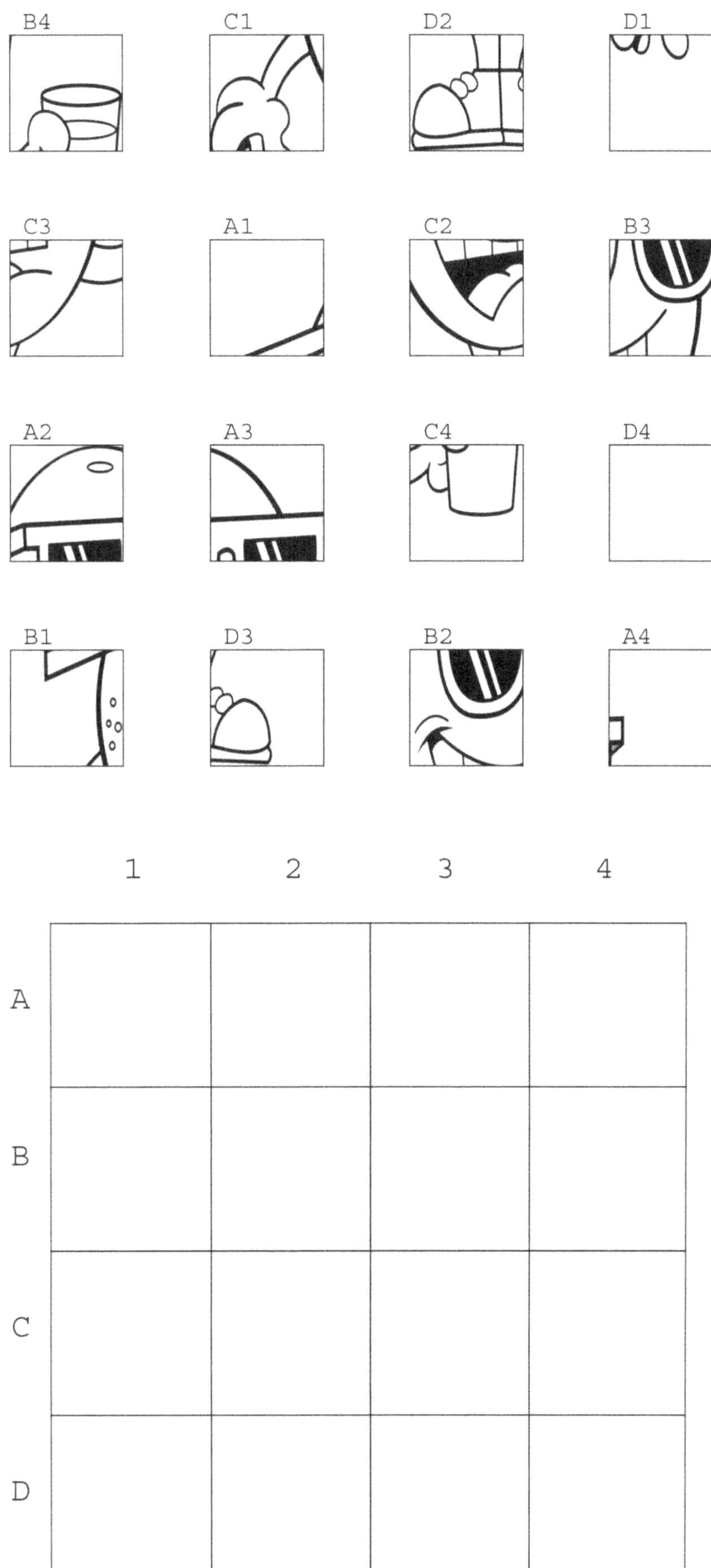

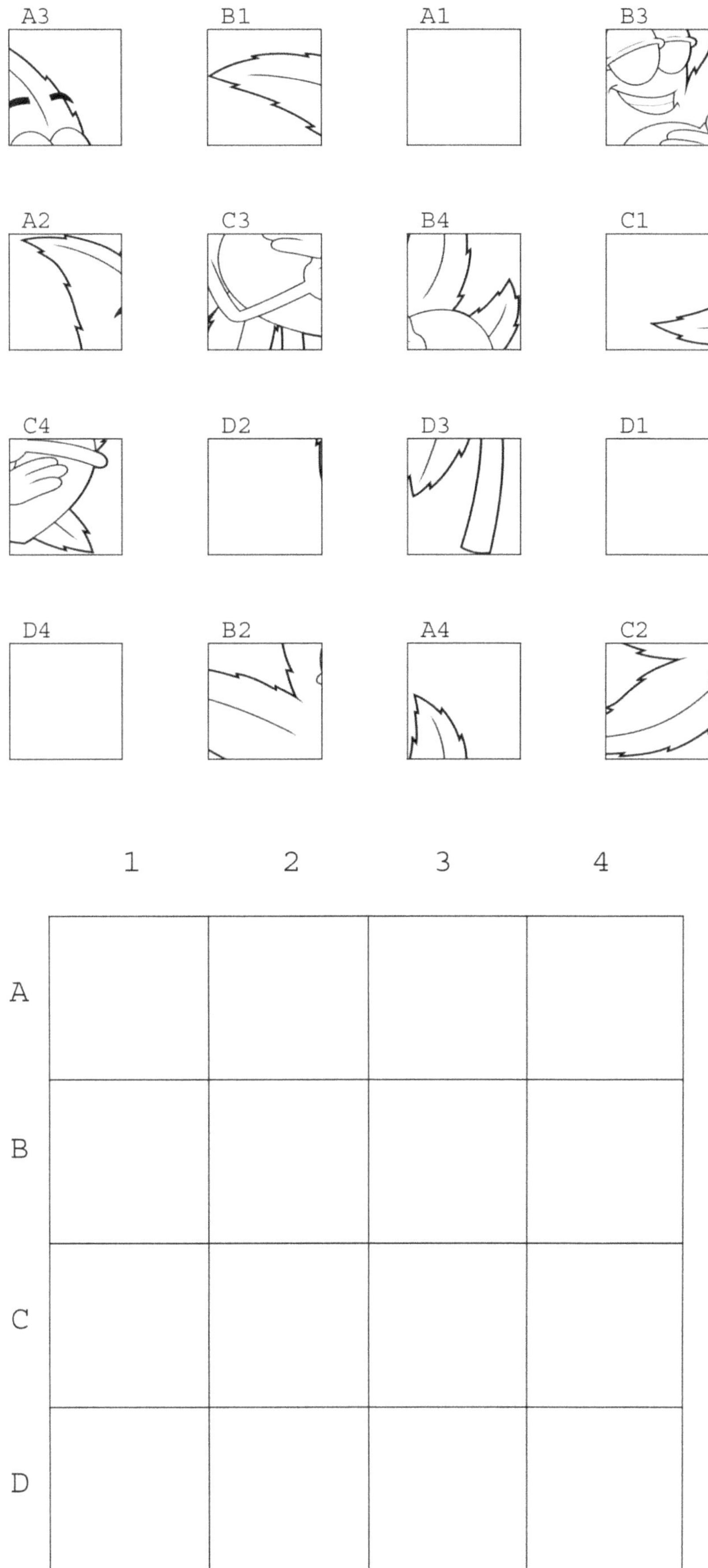

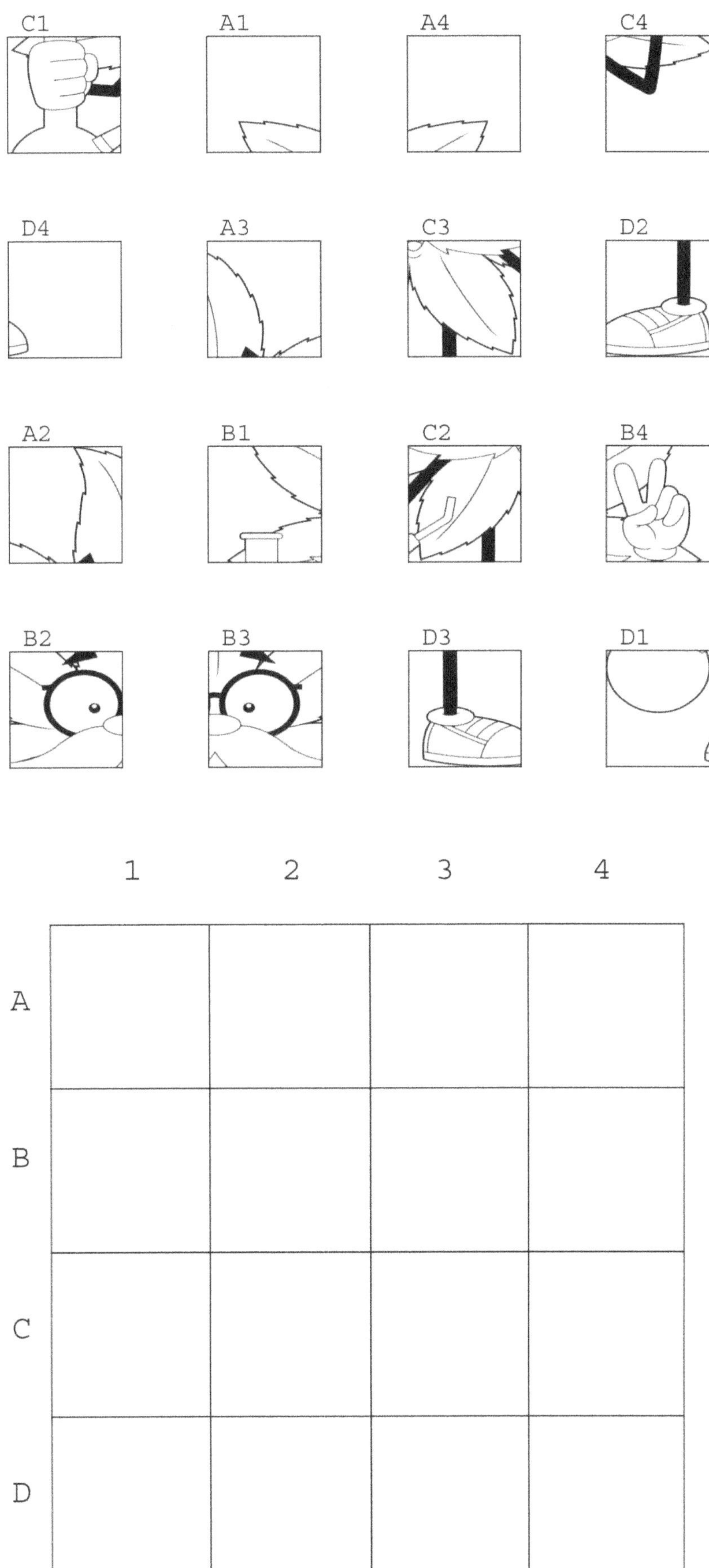

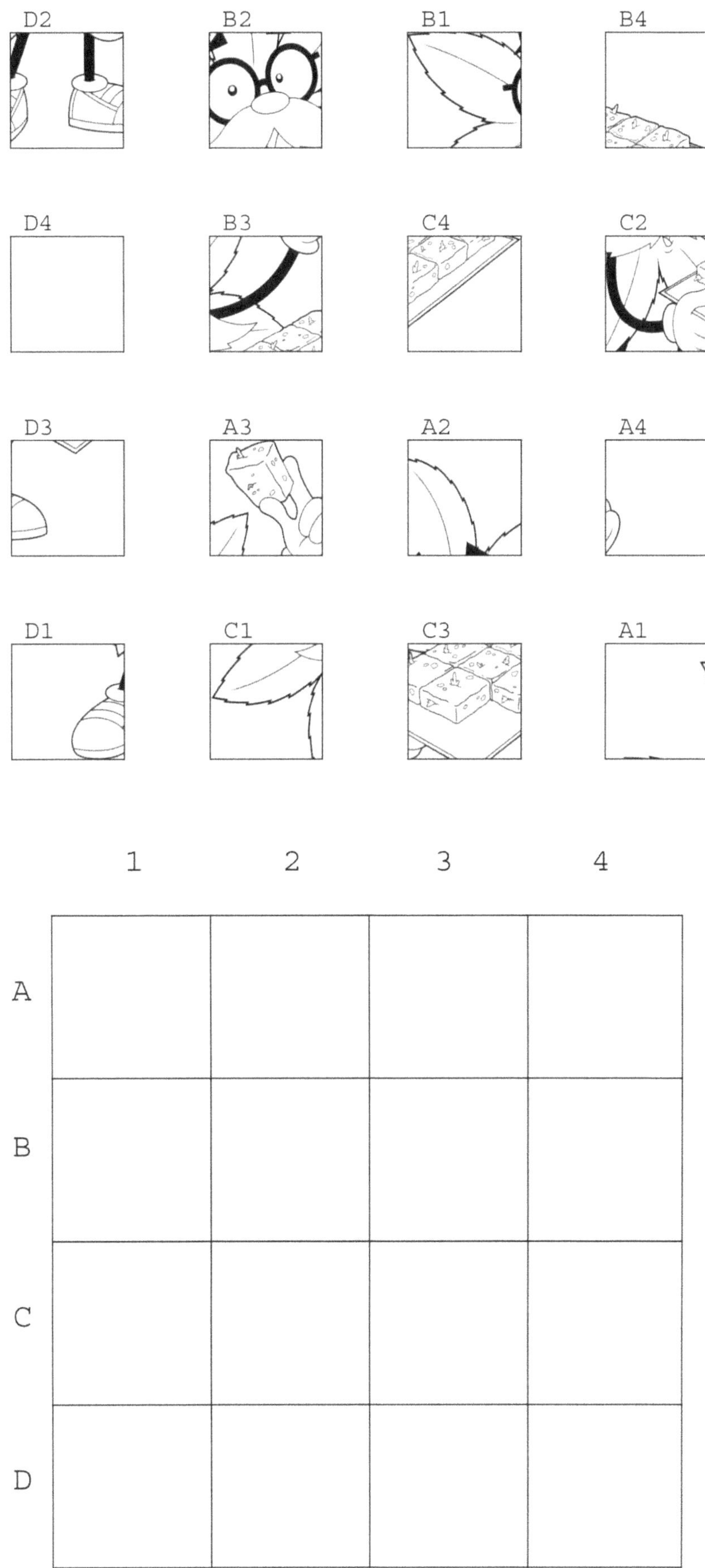

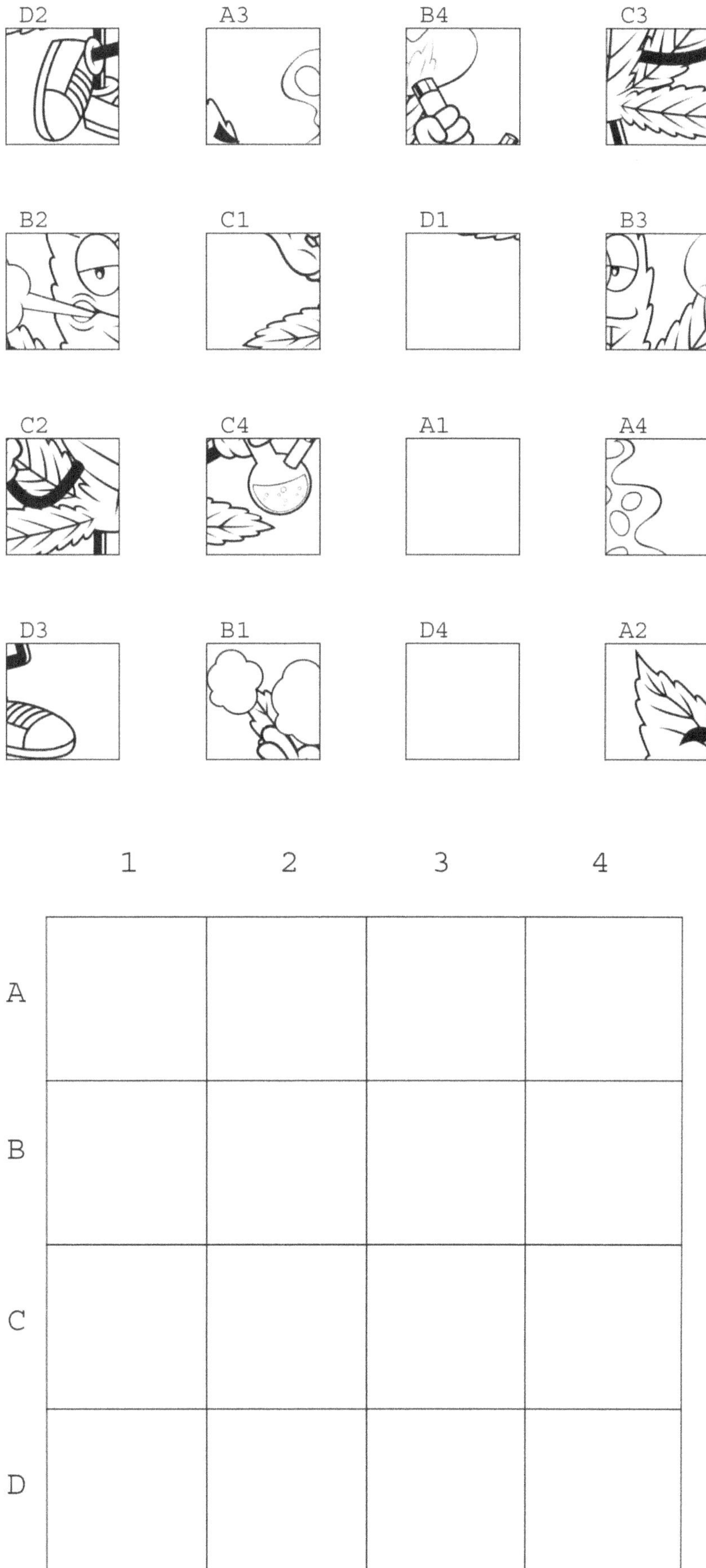

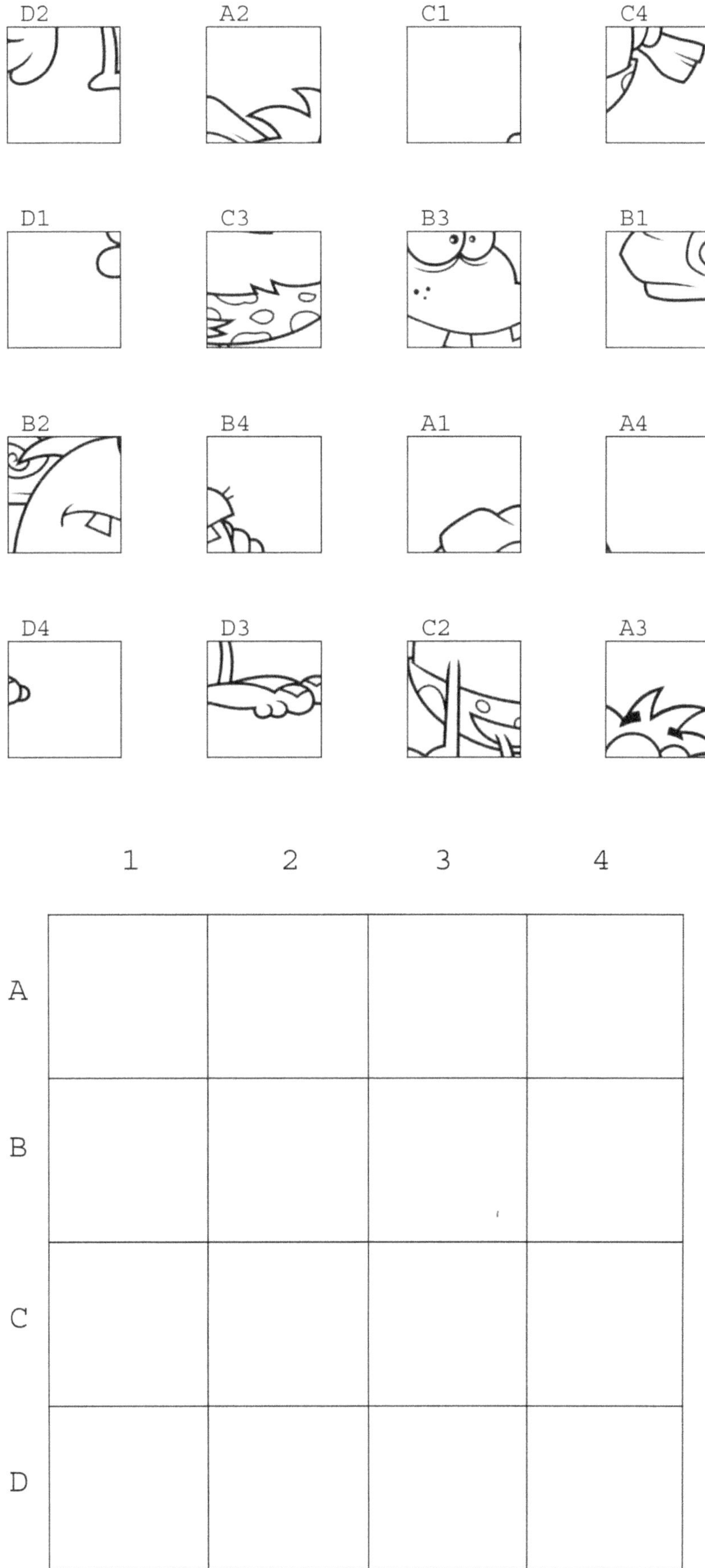

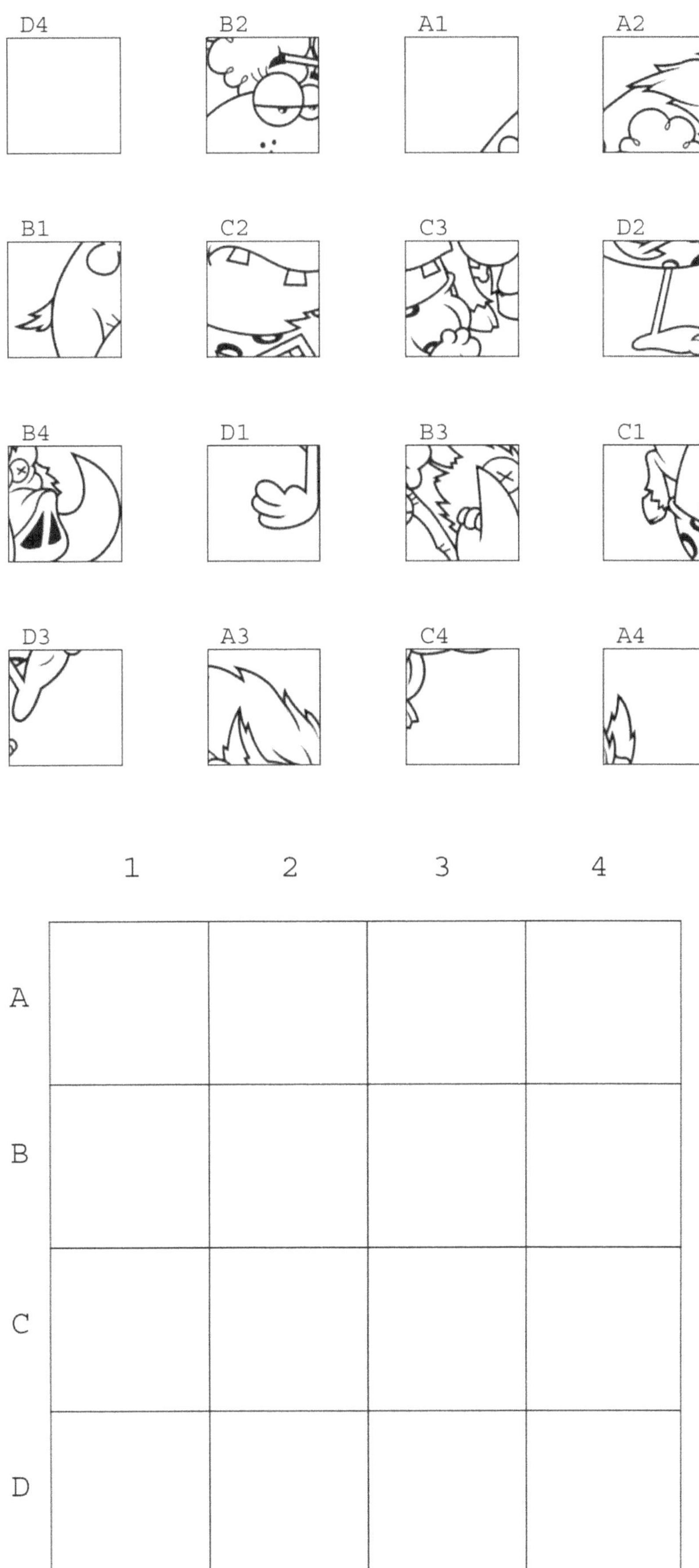

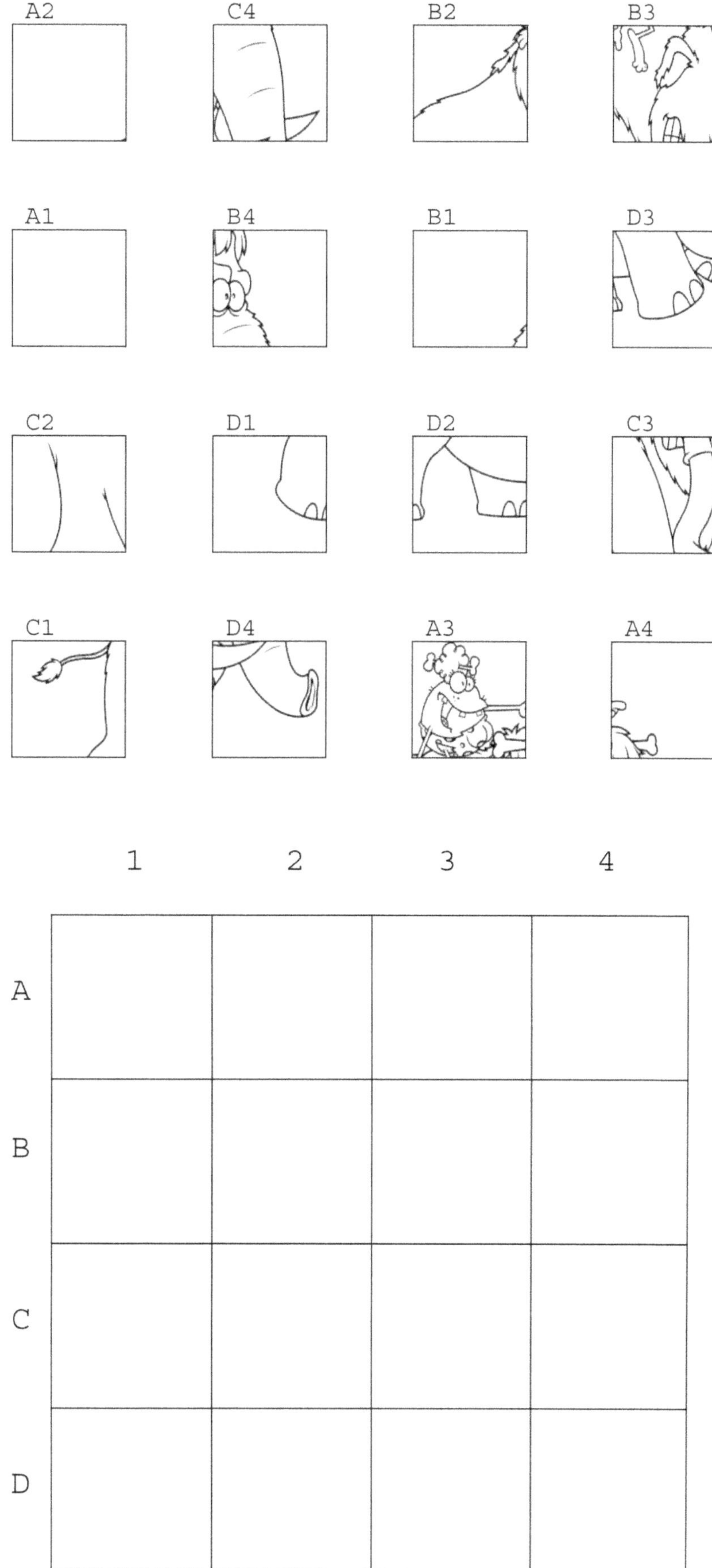

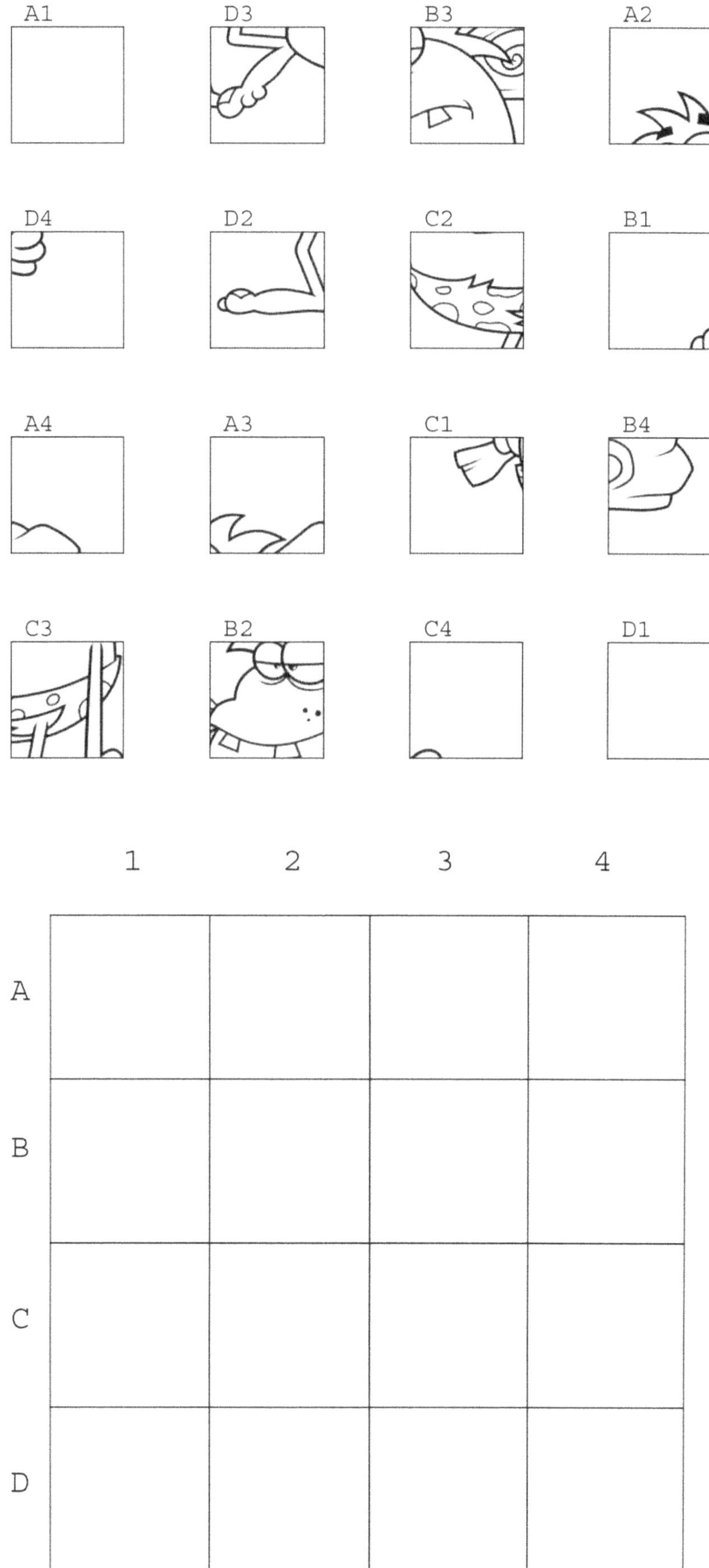

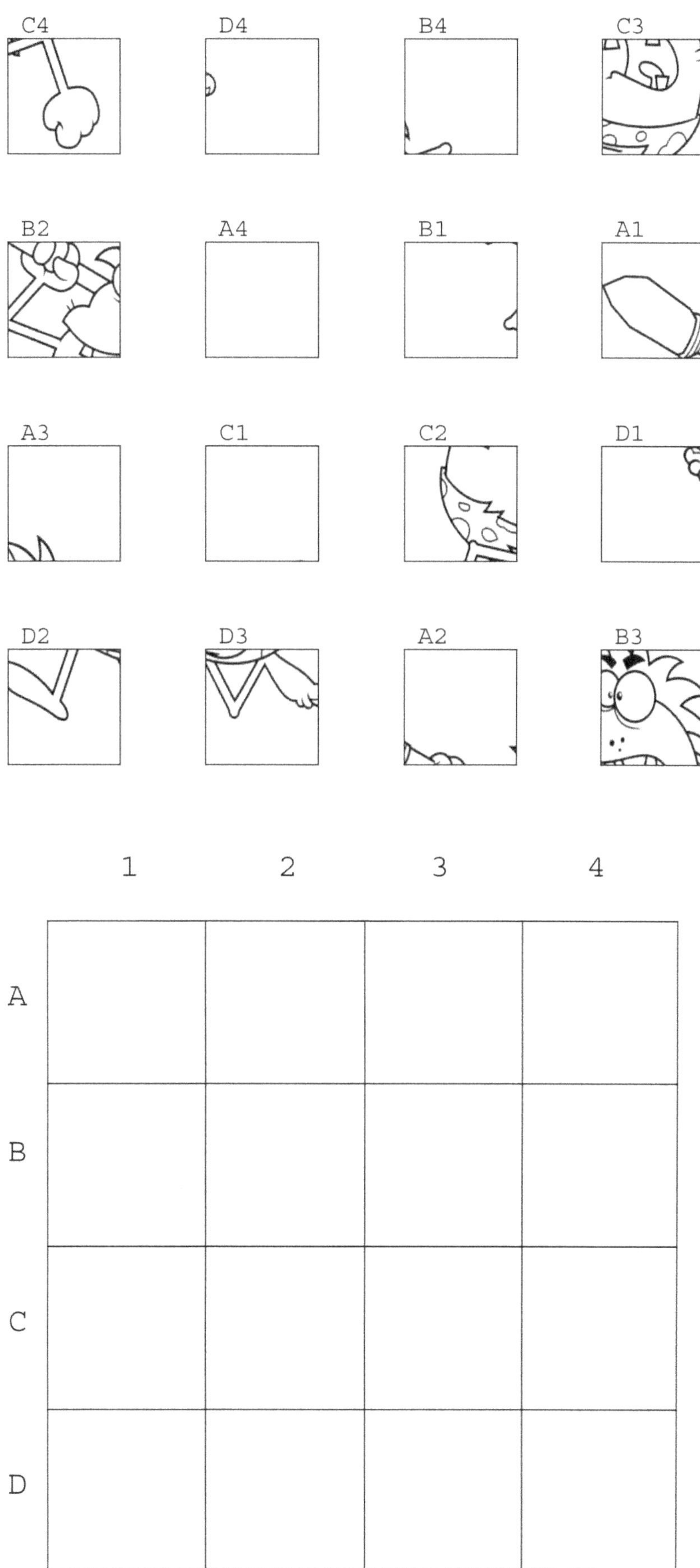

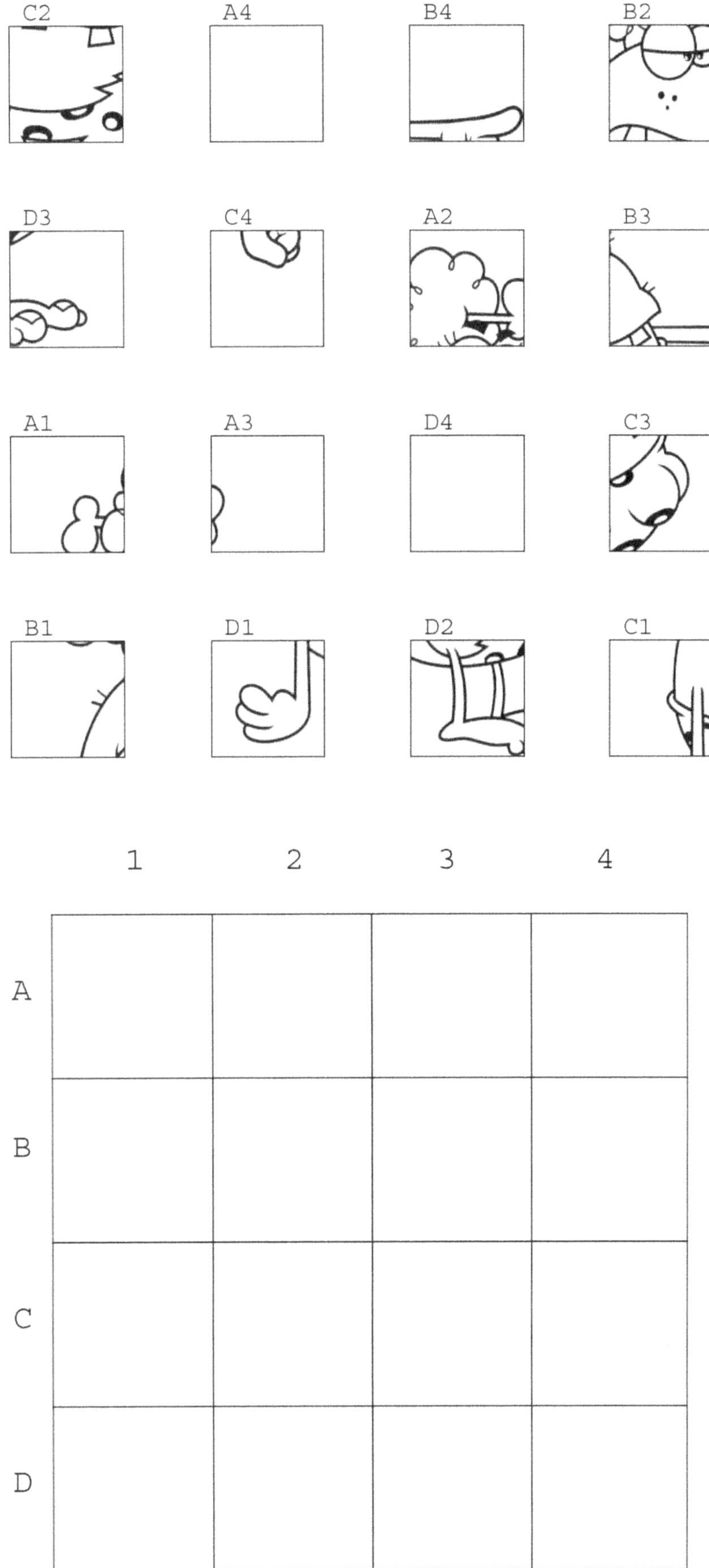

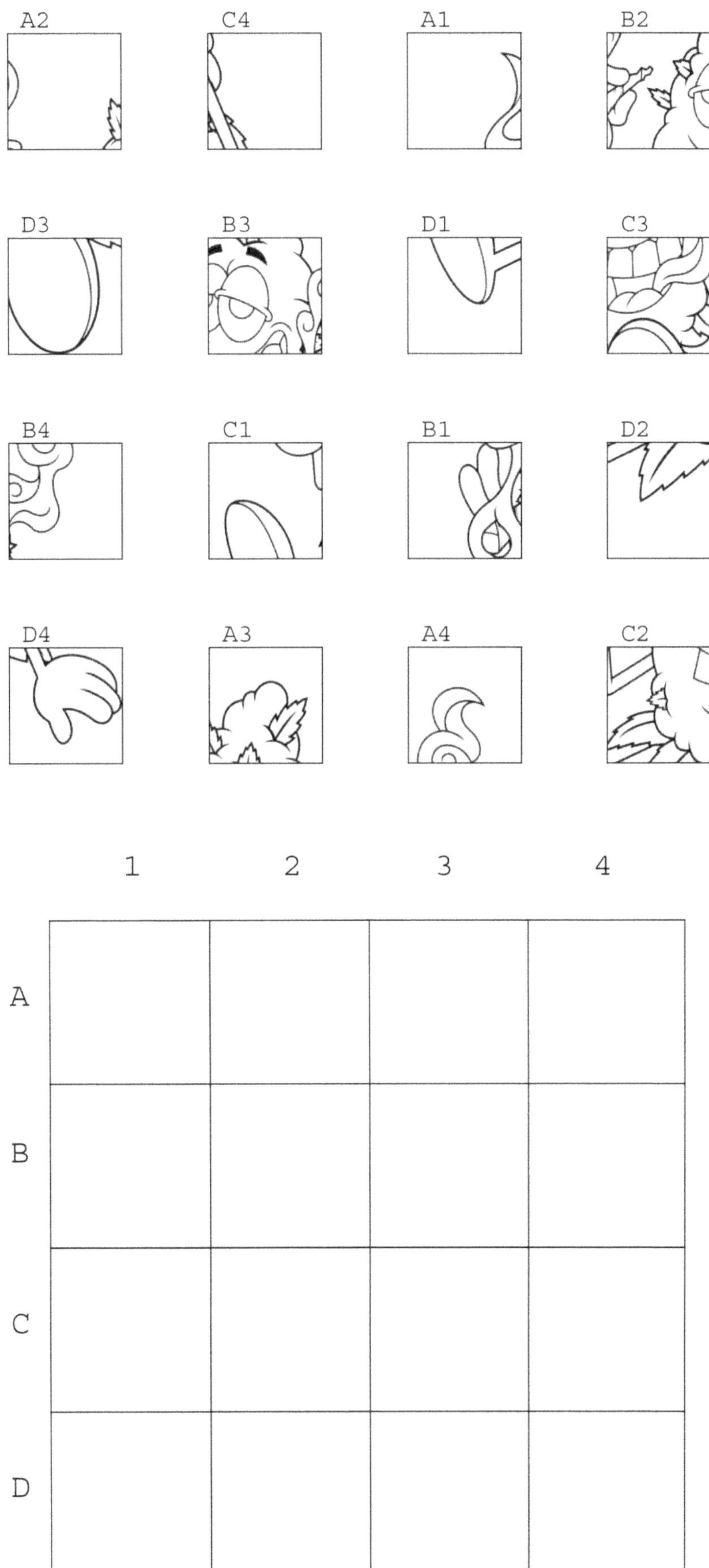

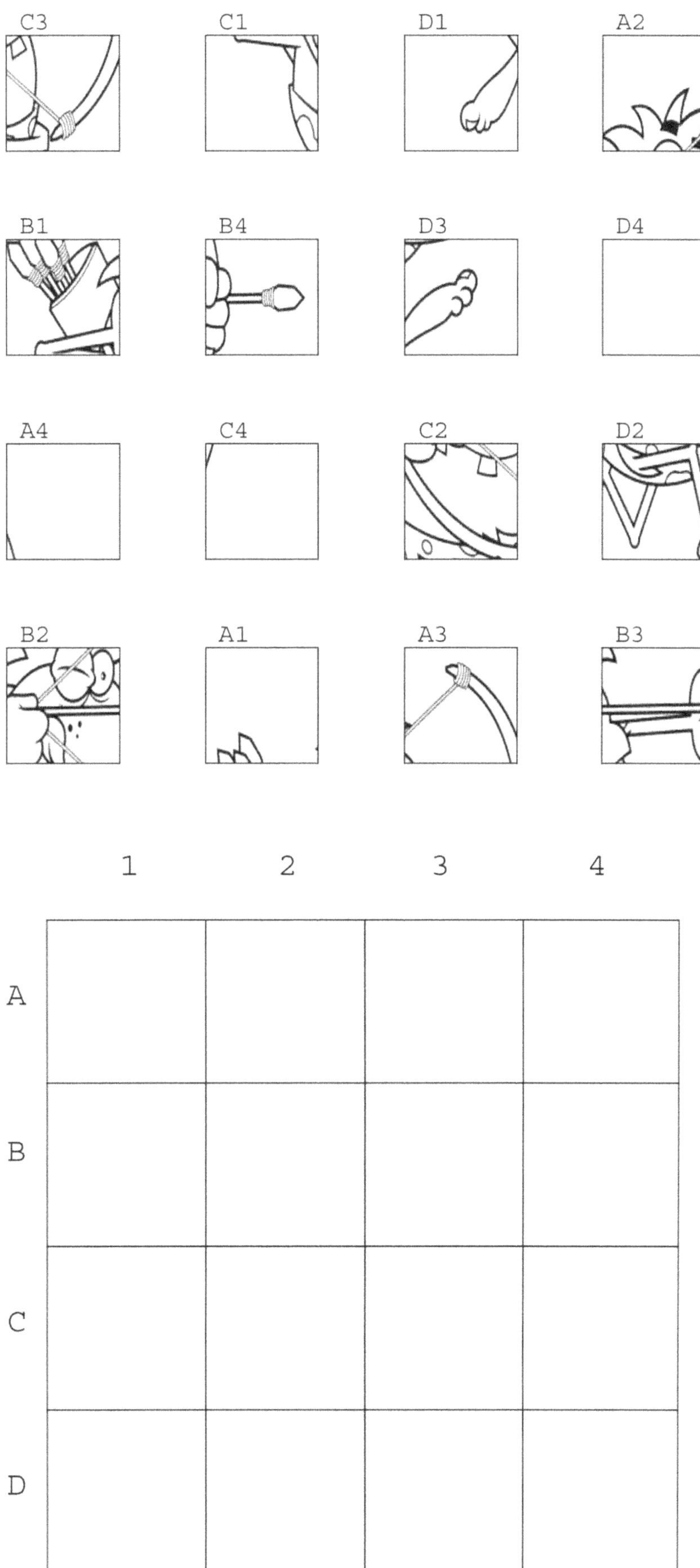

C3
C1
D1
A2
B1
B4
D3
D4
A4
C4
C2
D2
B2
A1
A3
B3
1
2
3
4
A
B
C
D

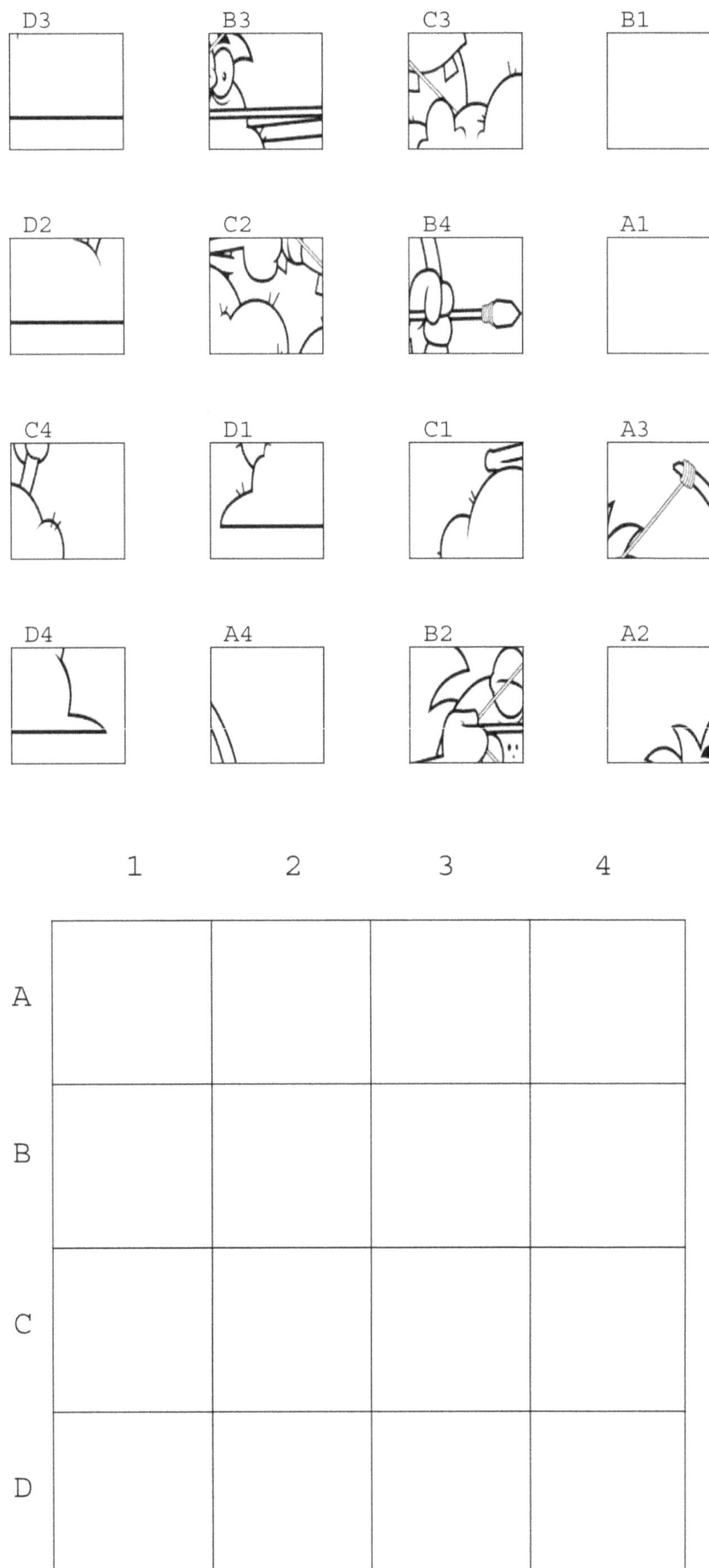

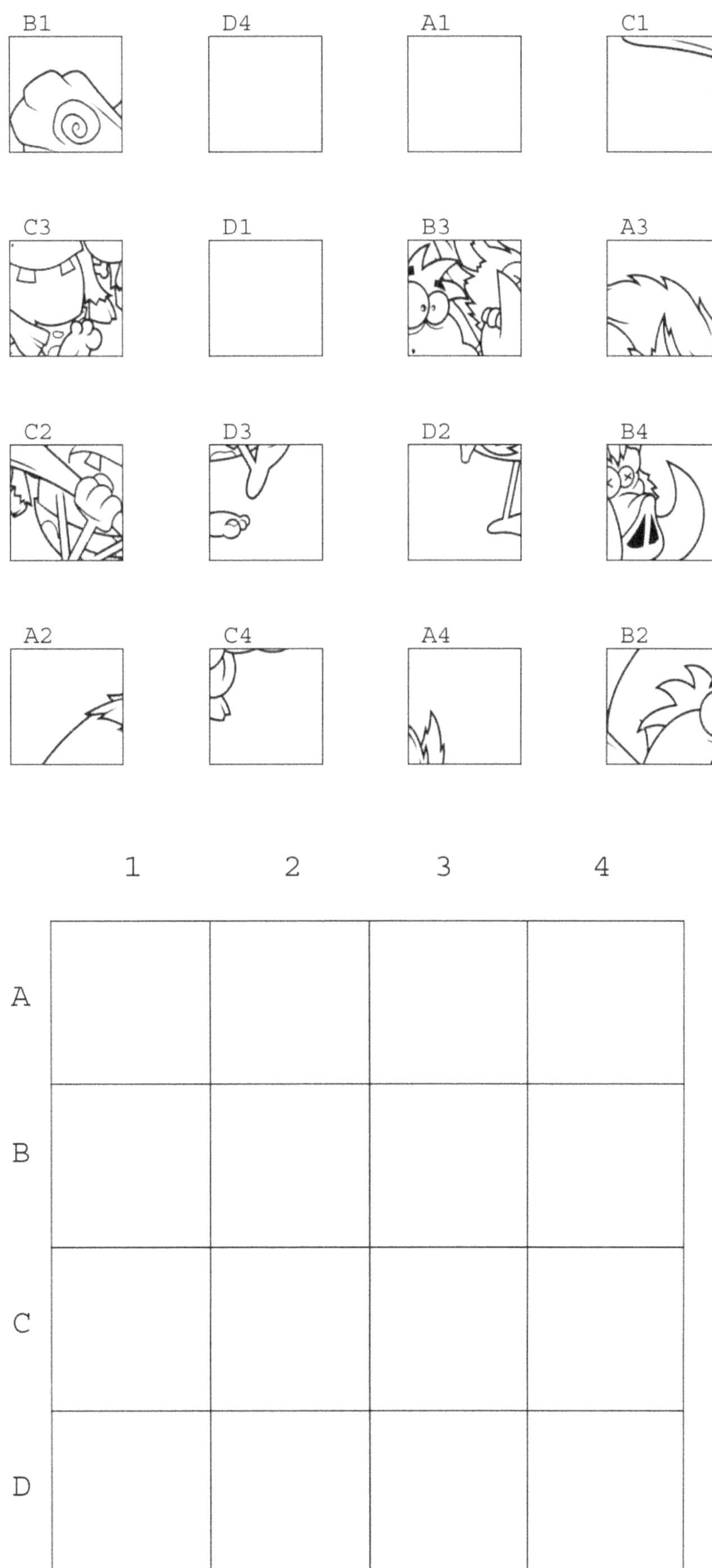

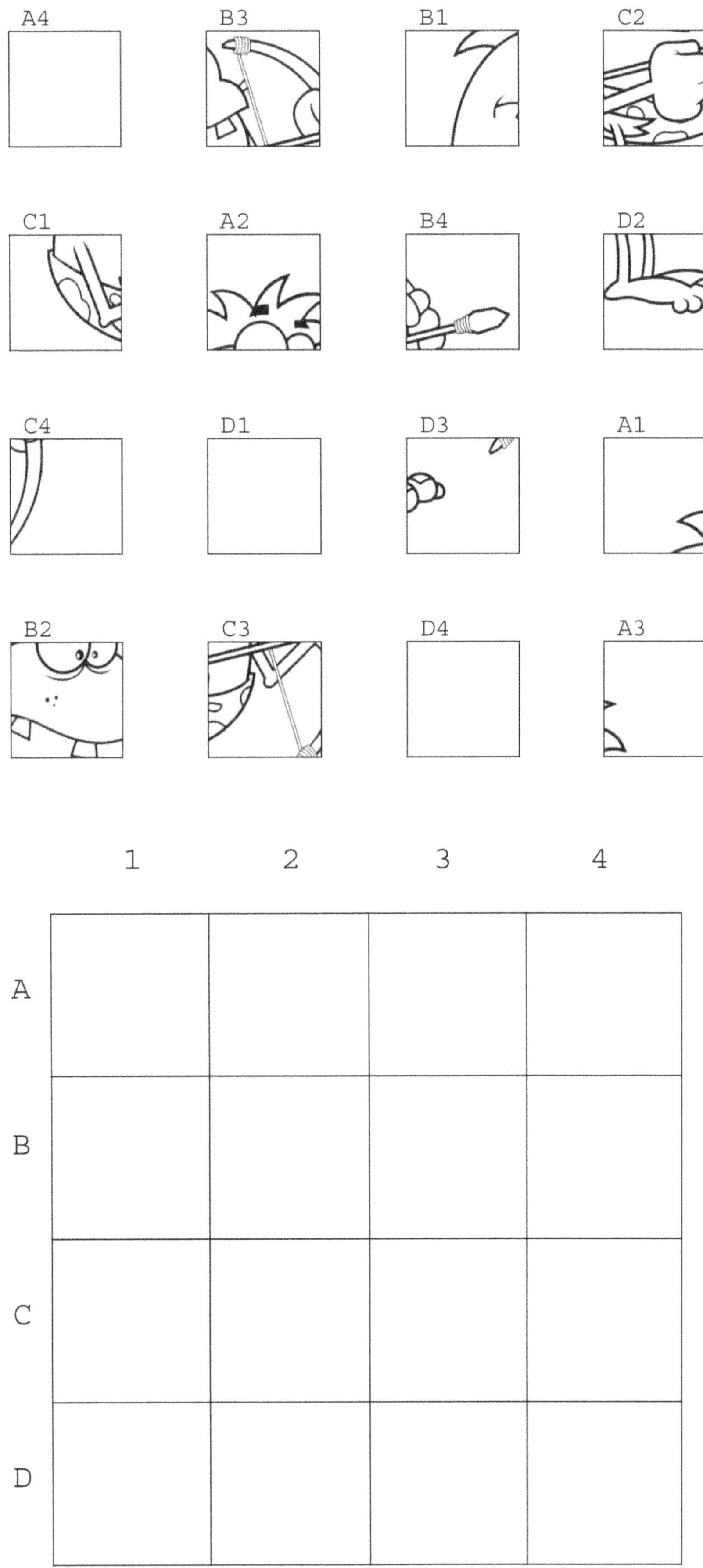

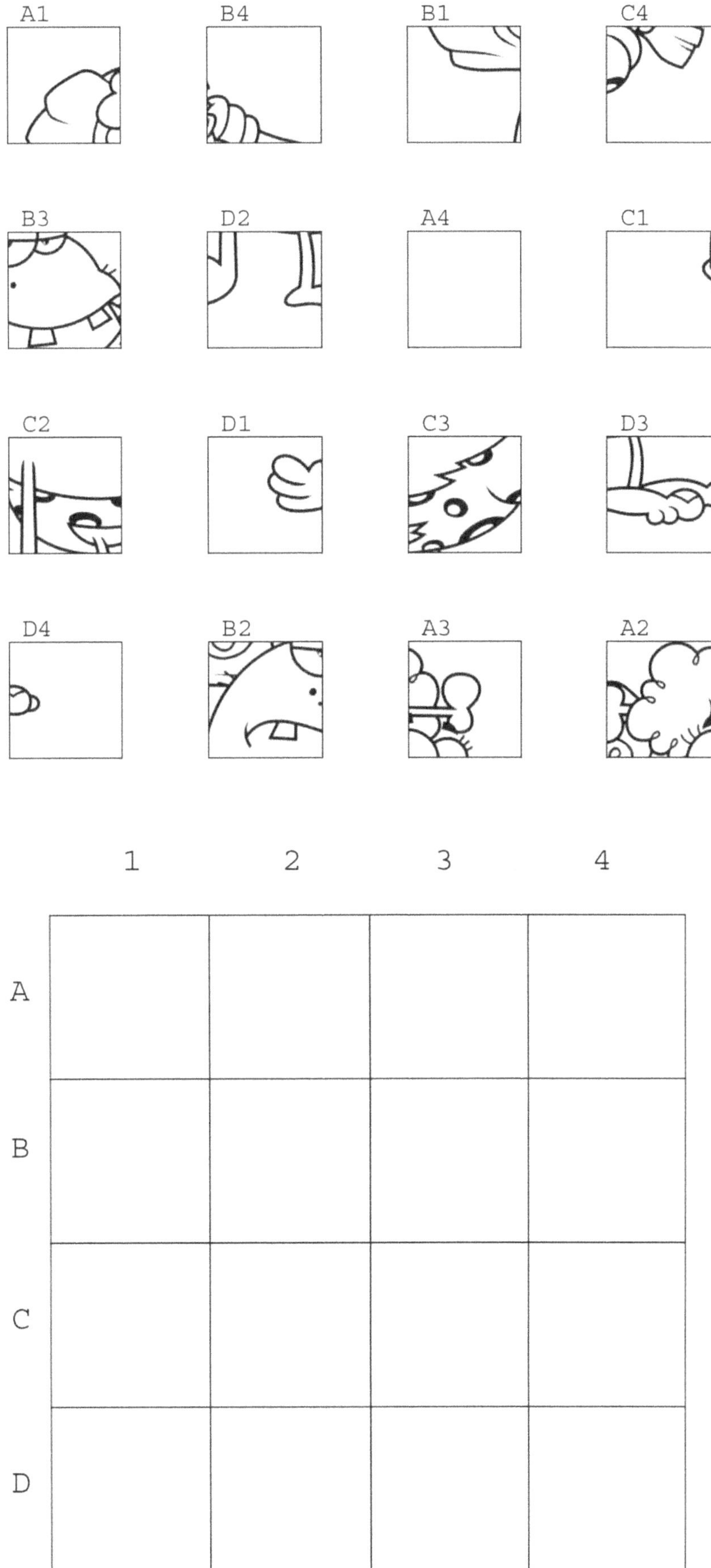

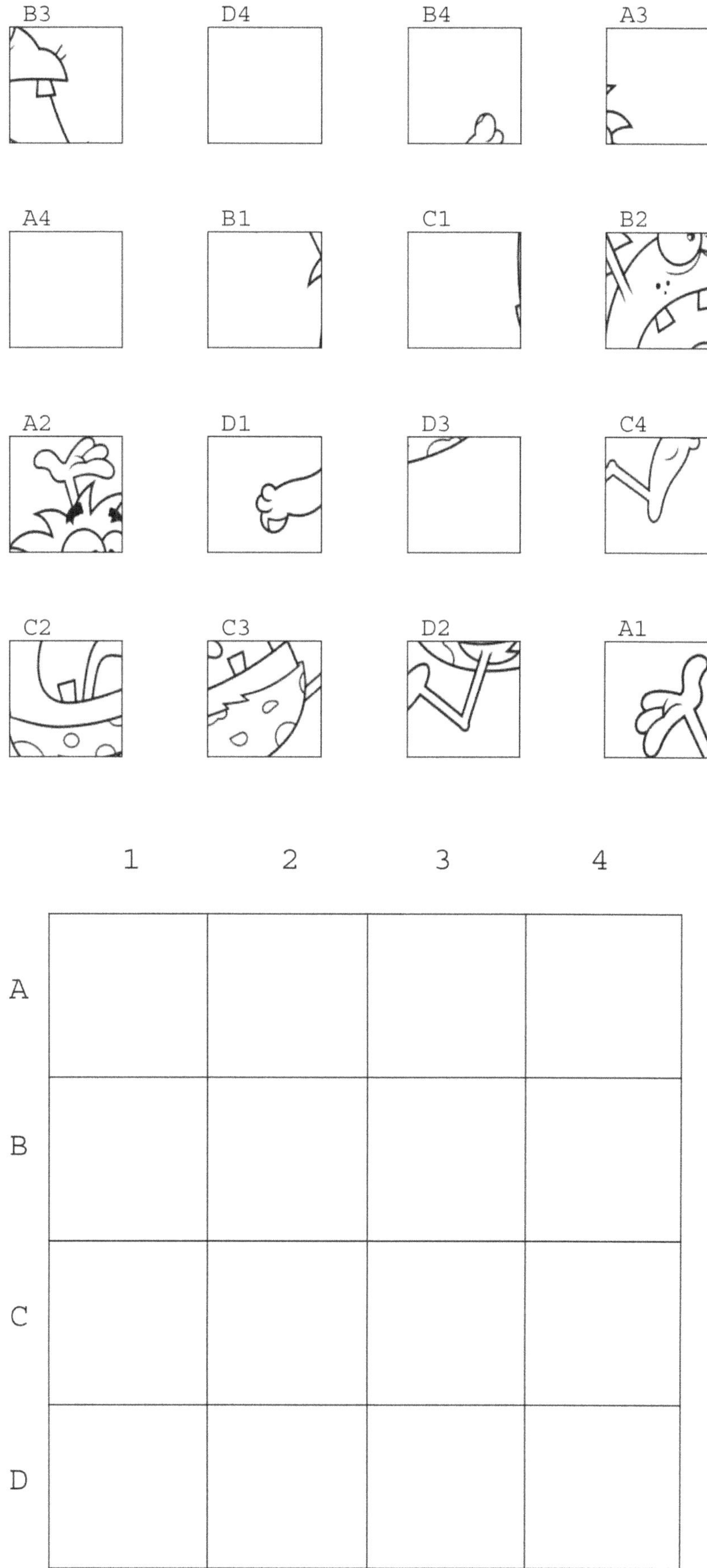

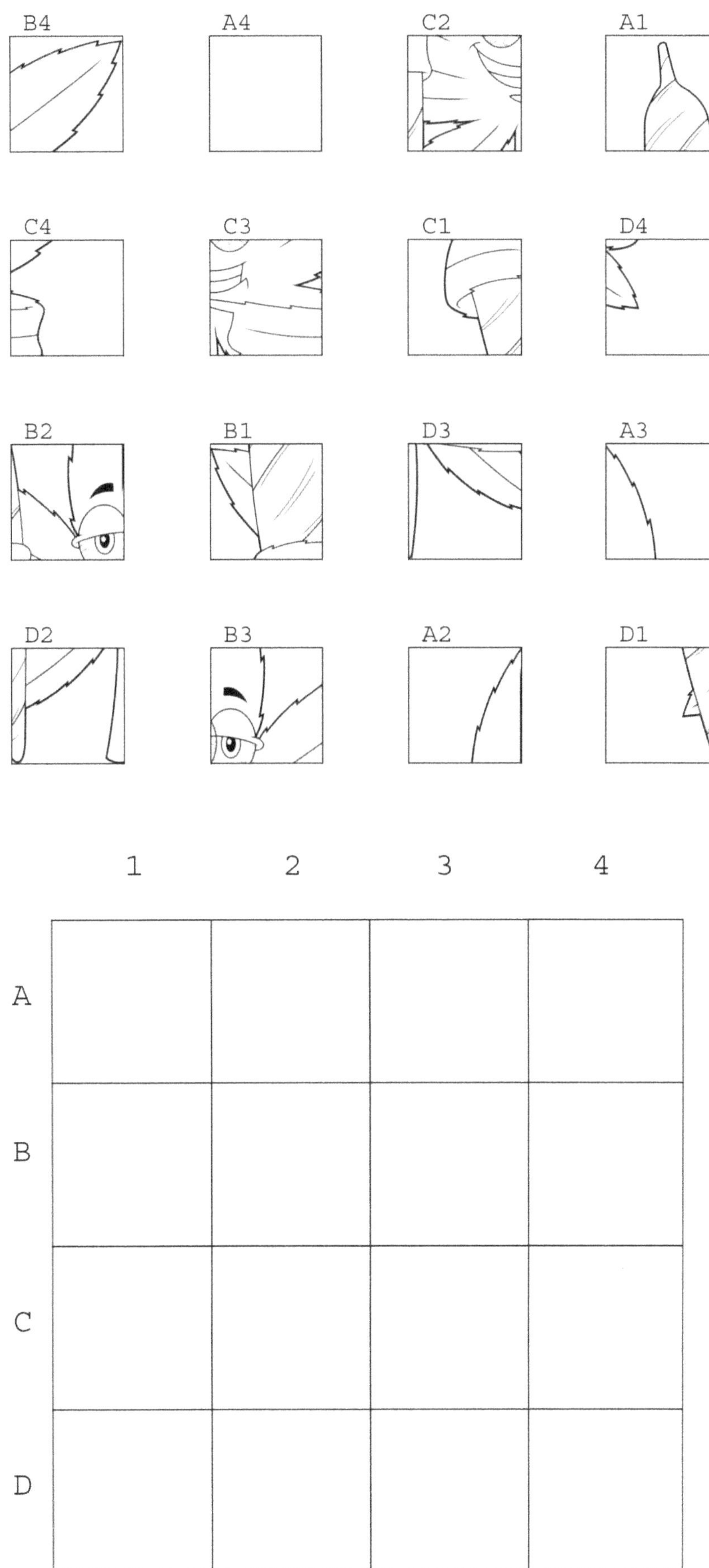

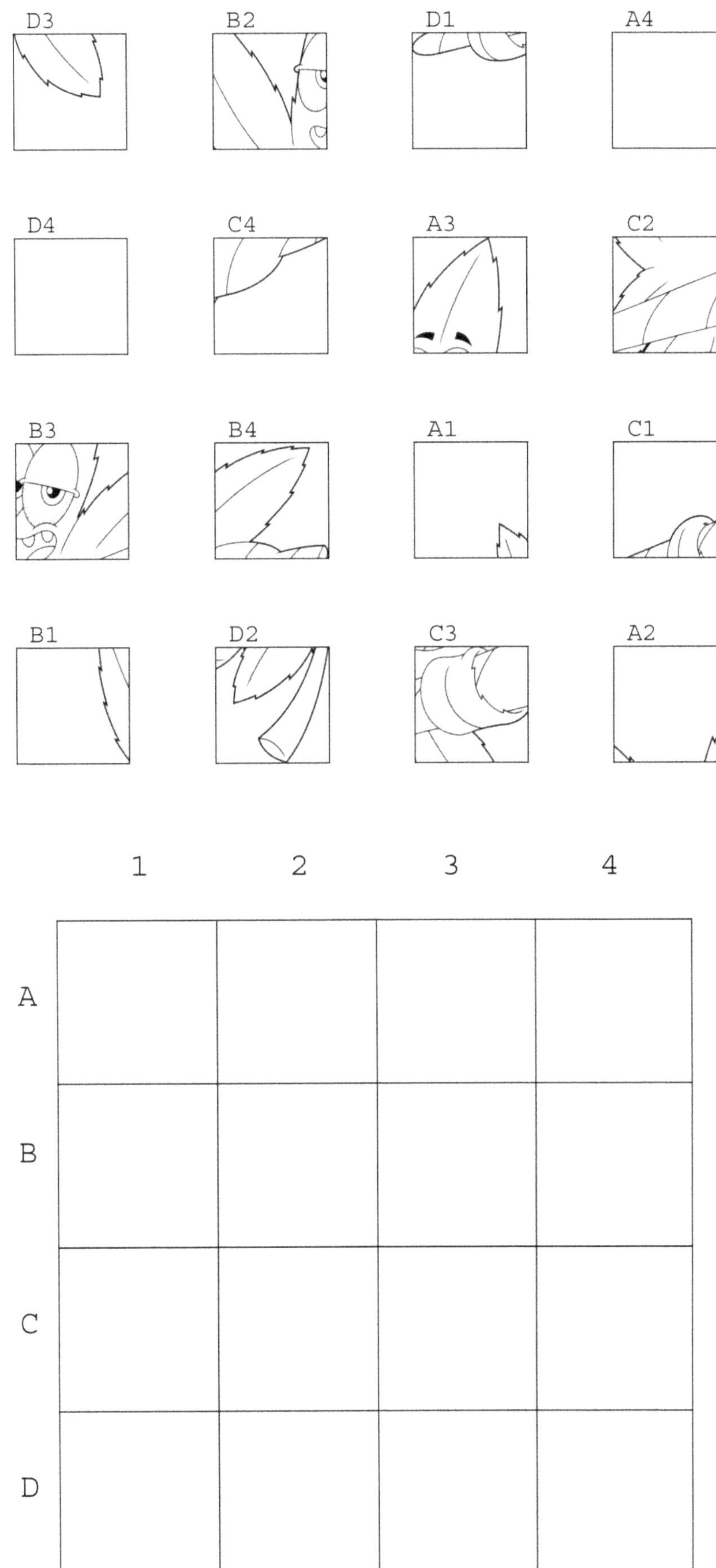

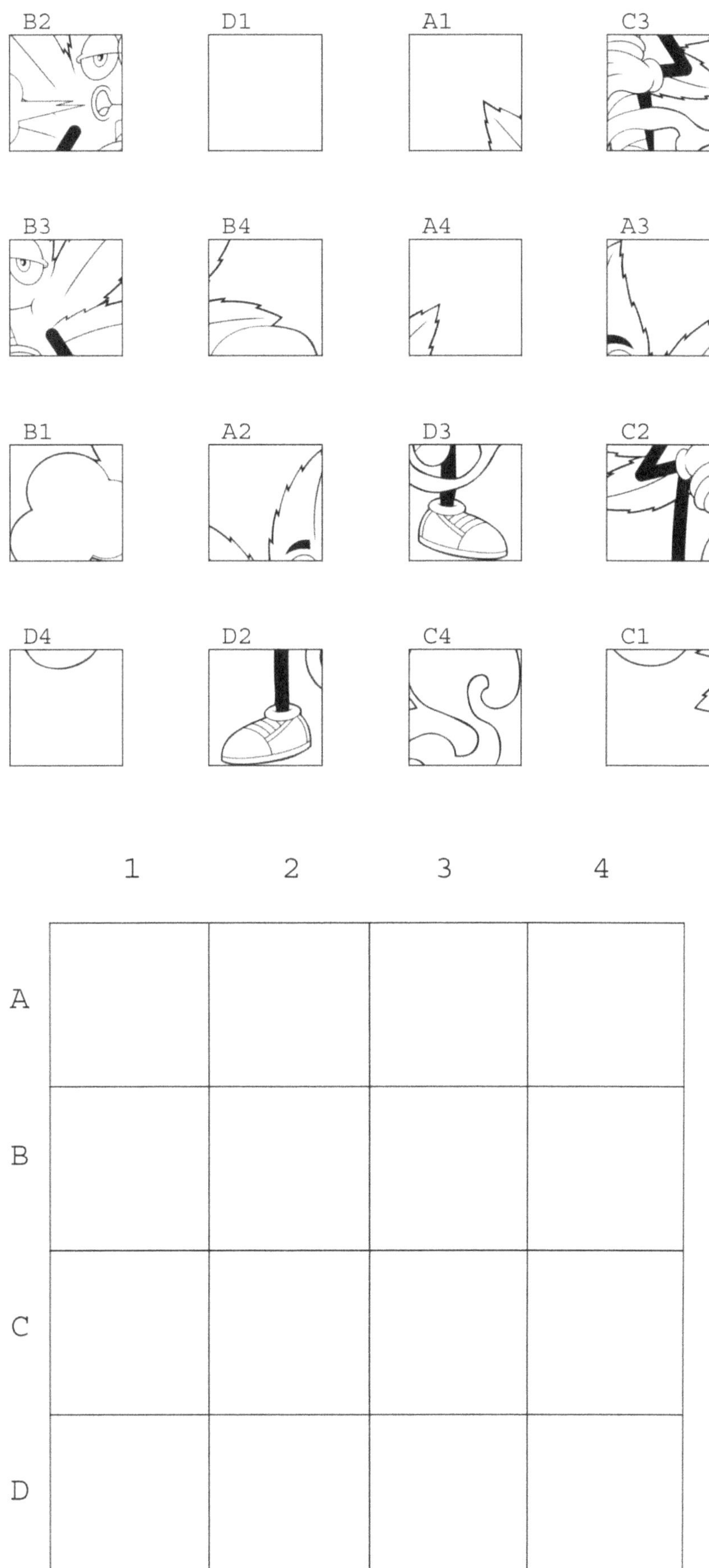

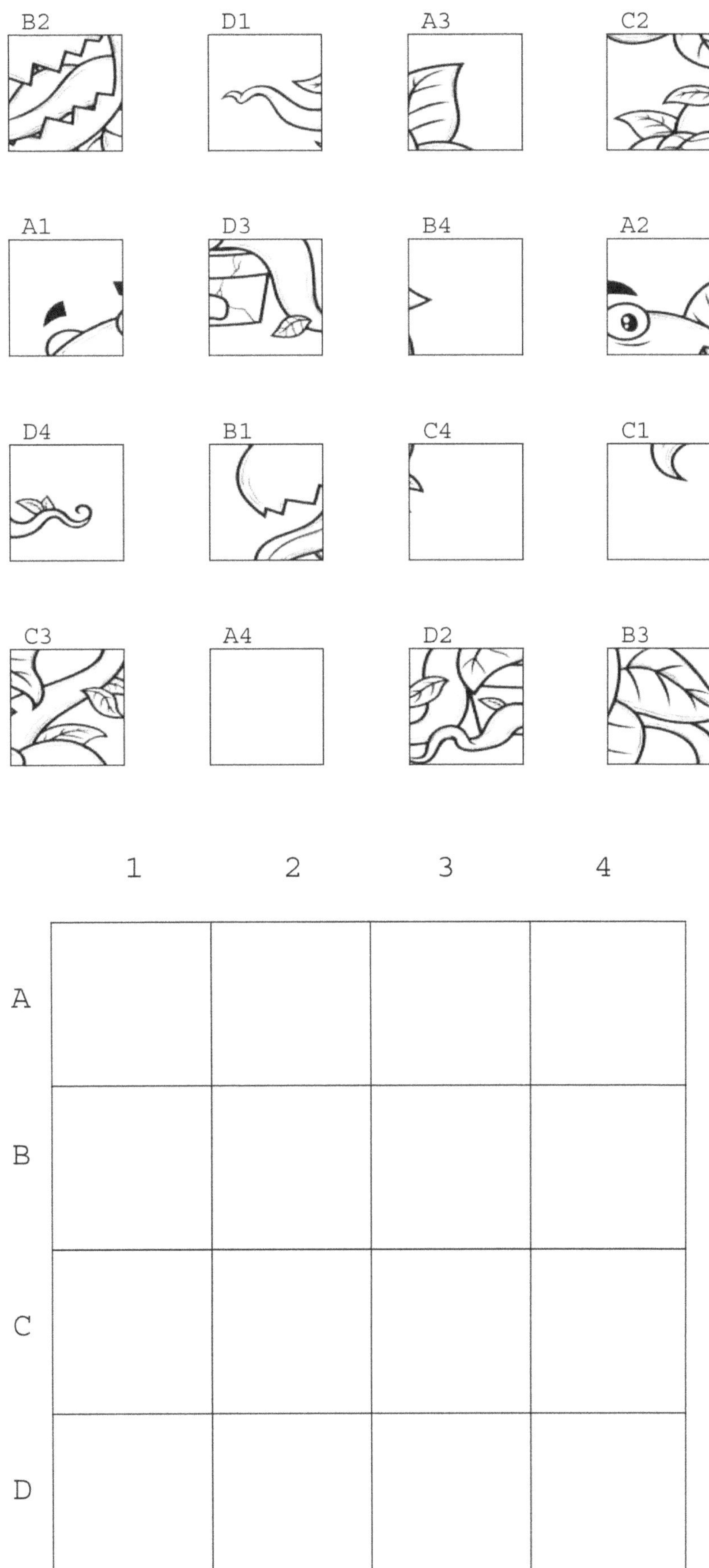

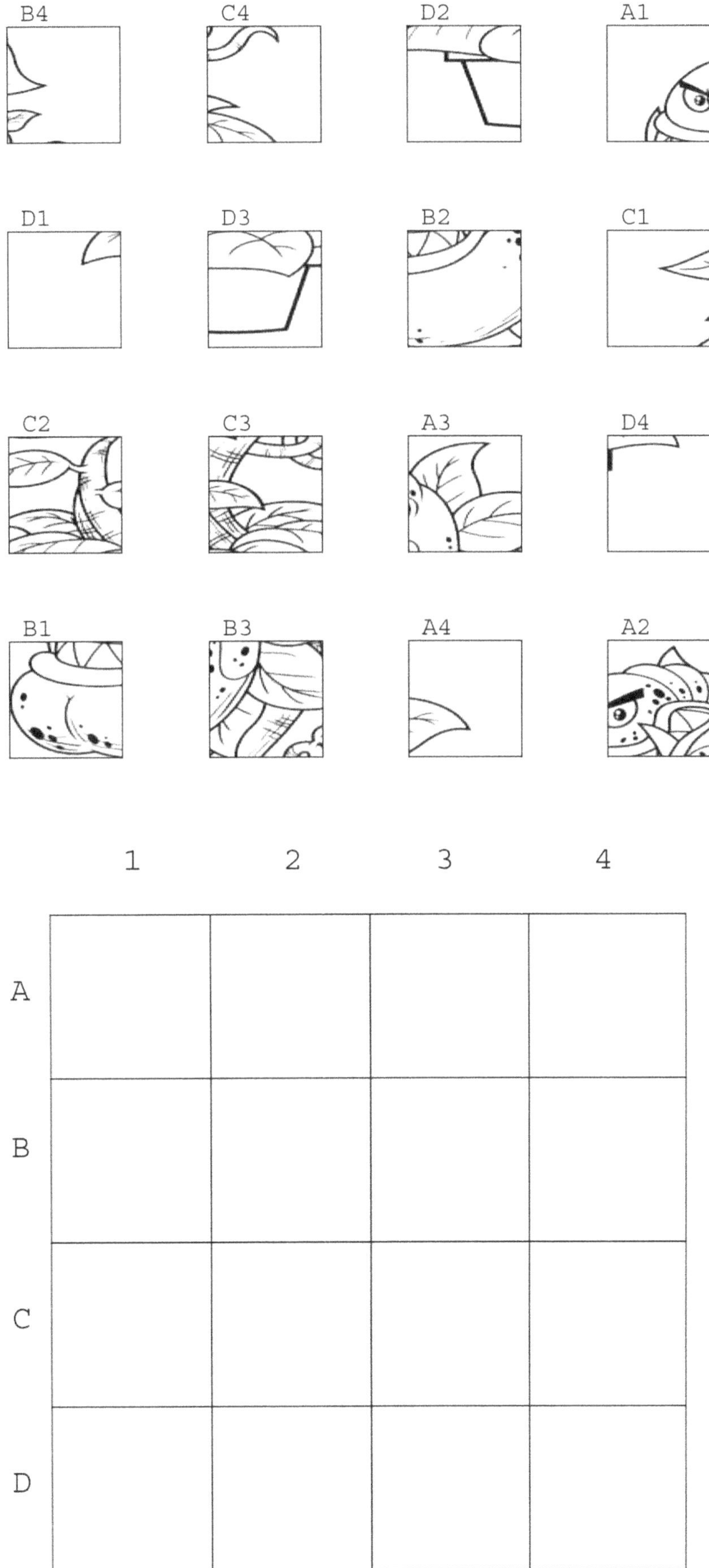

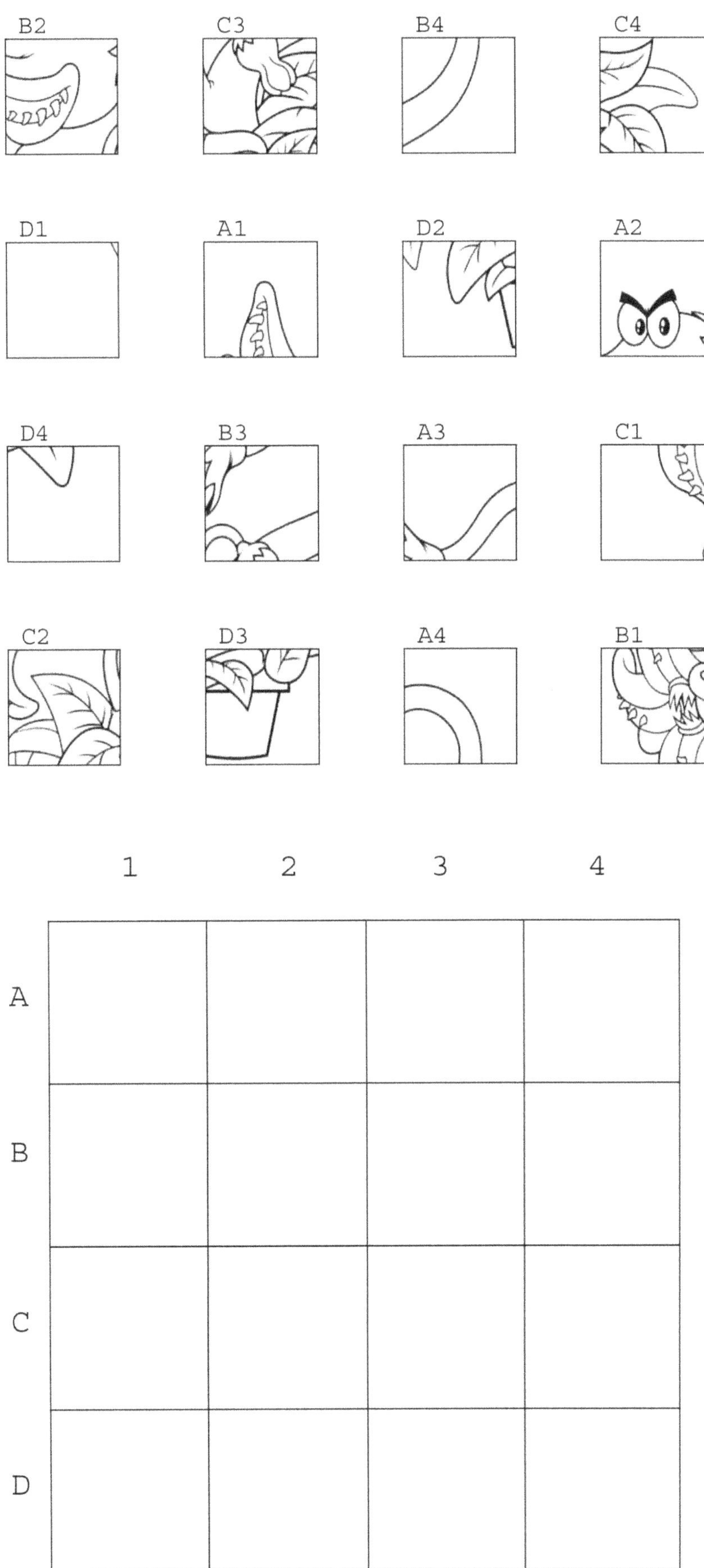

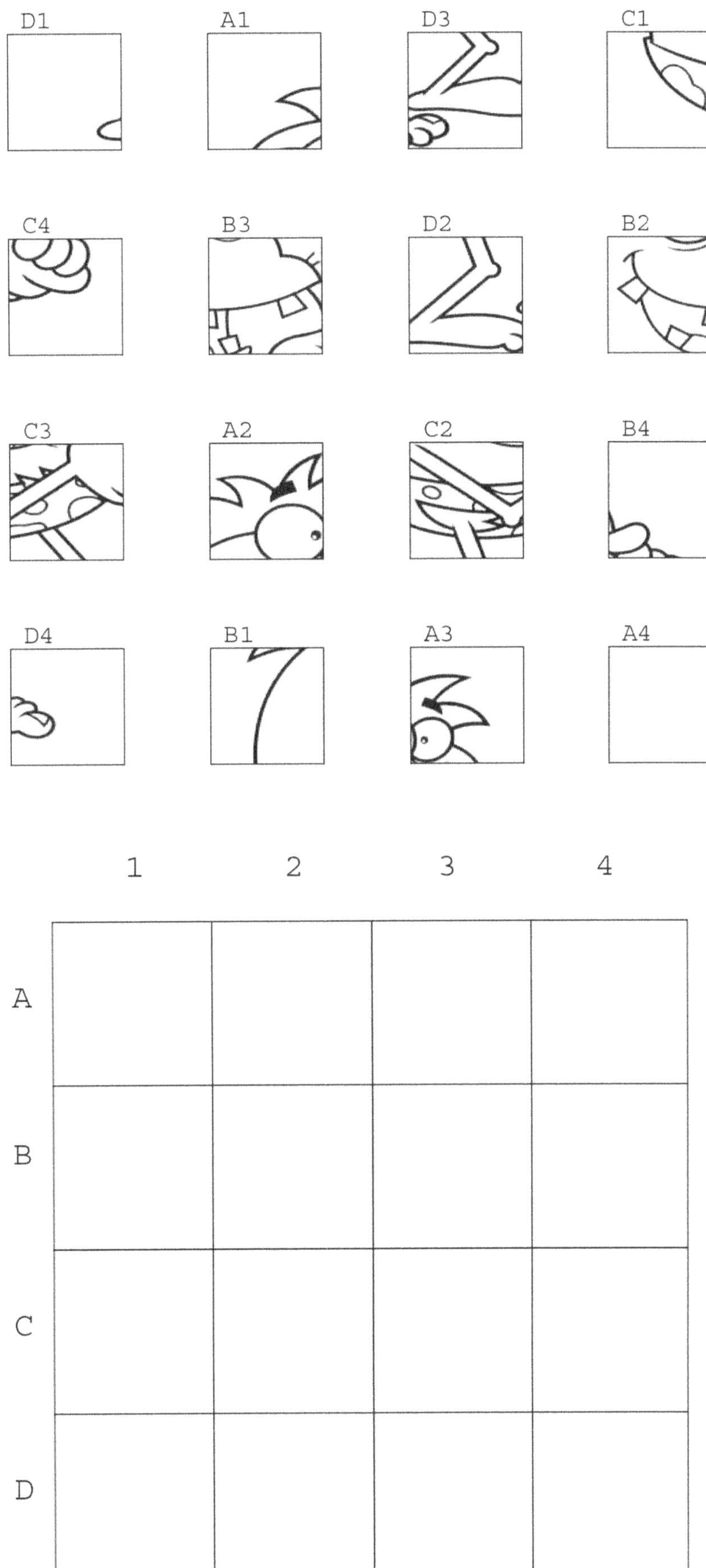

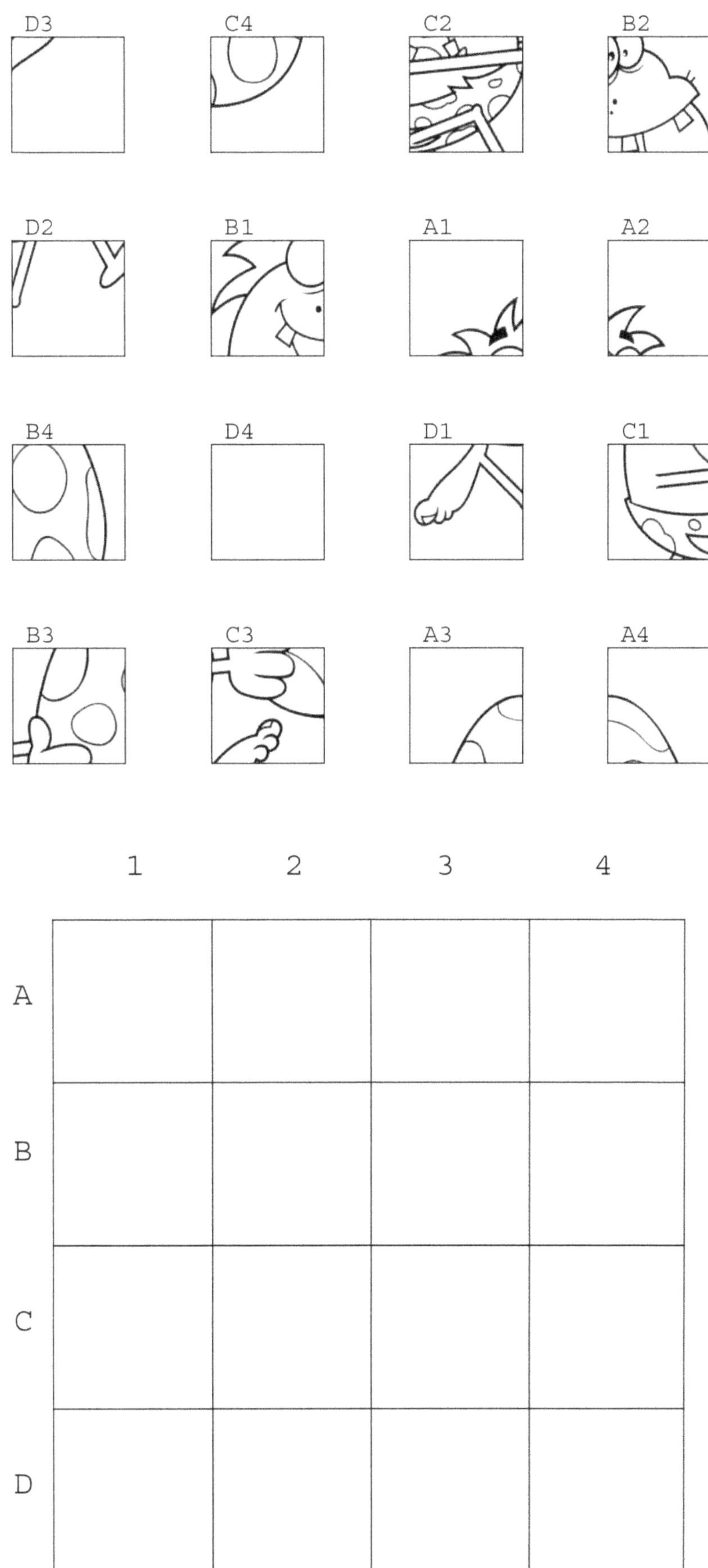

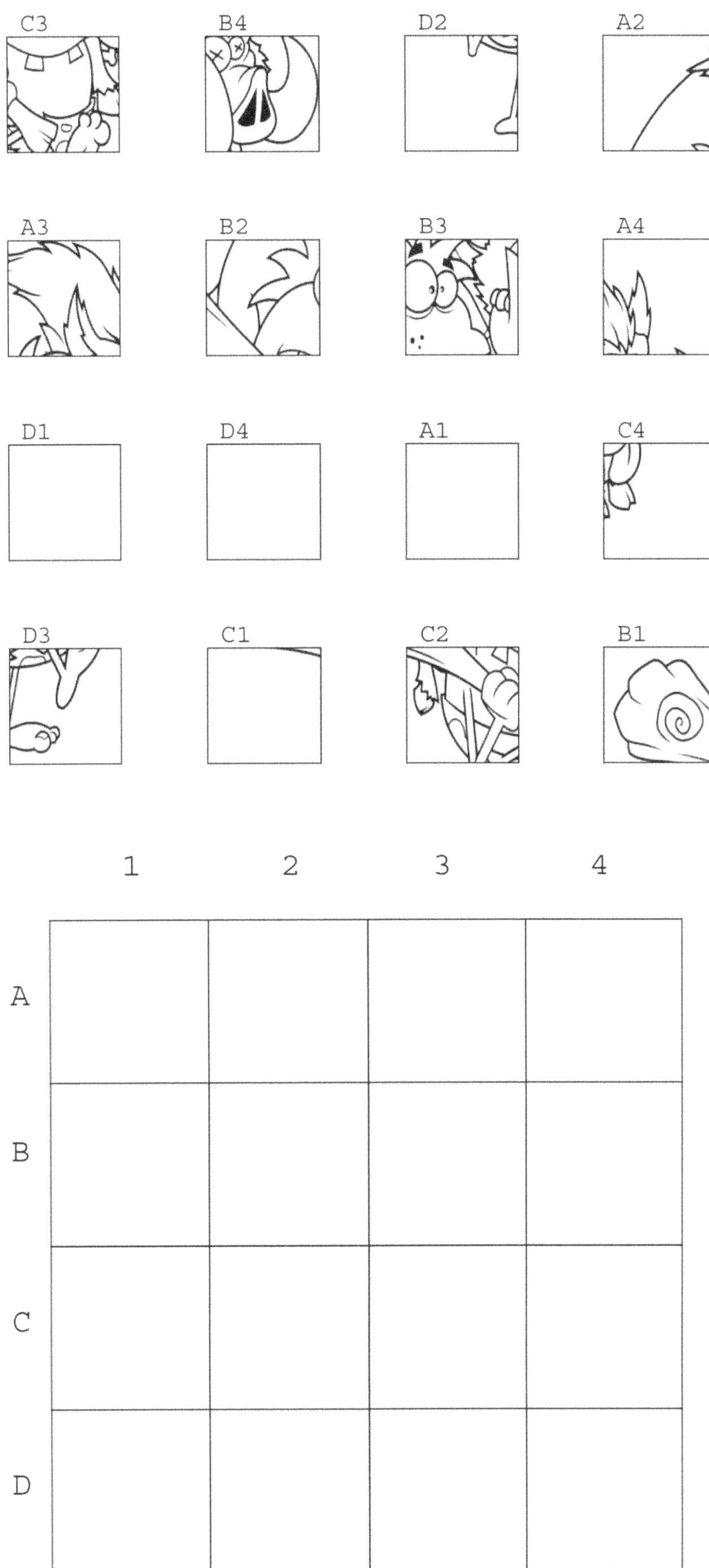

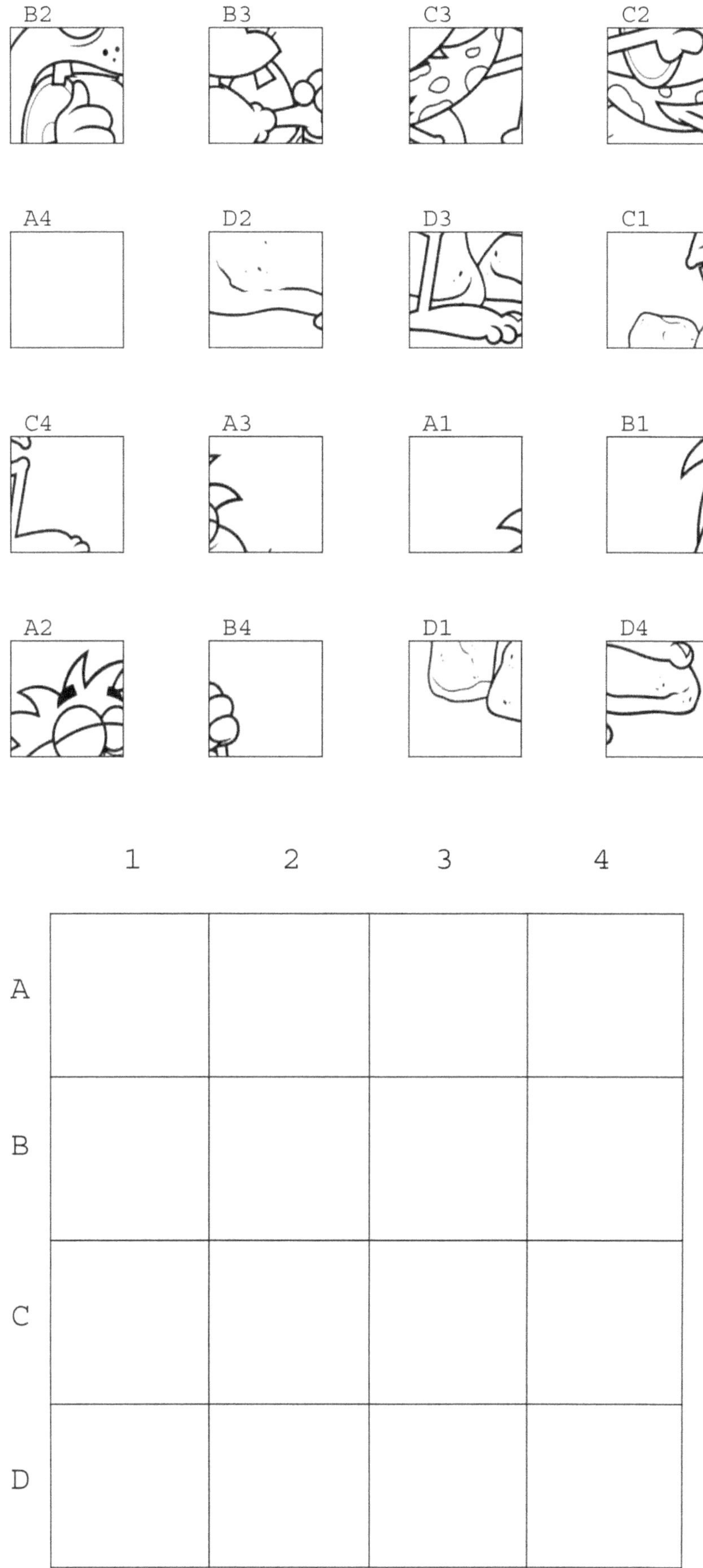

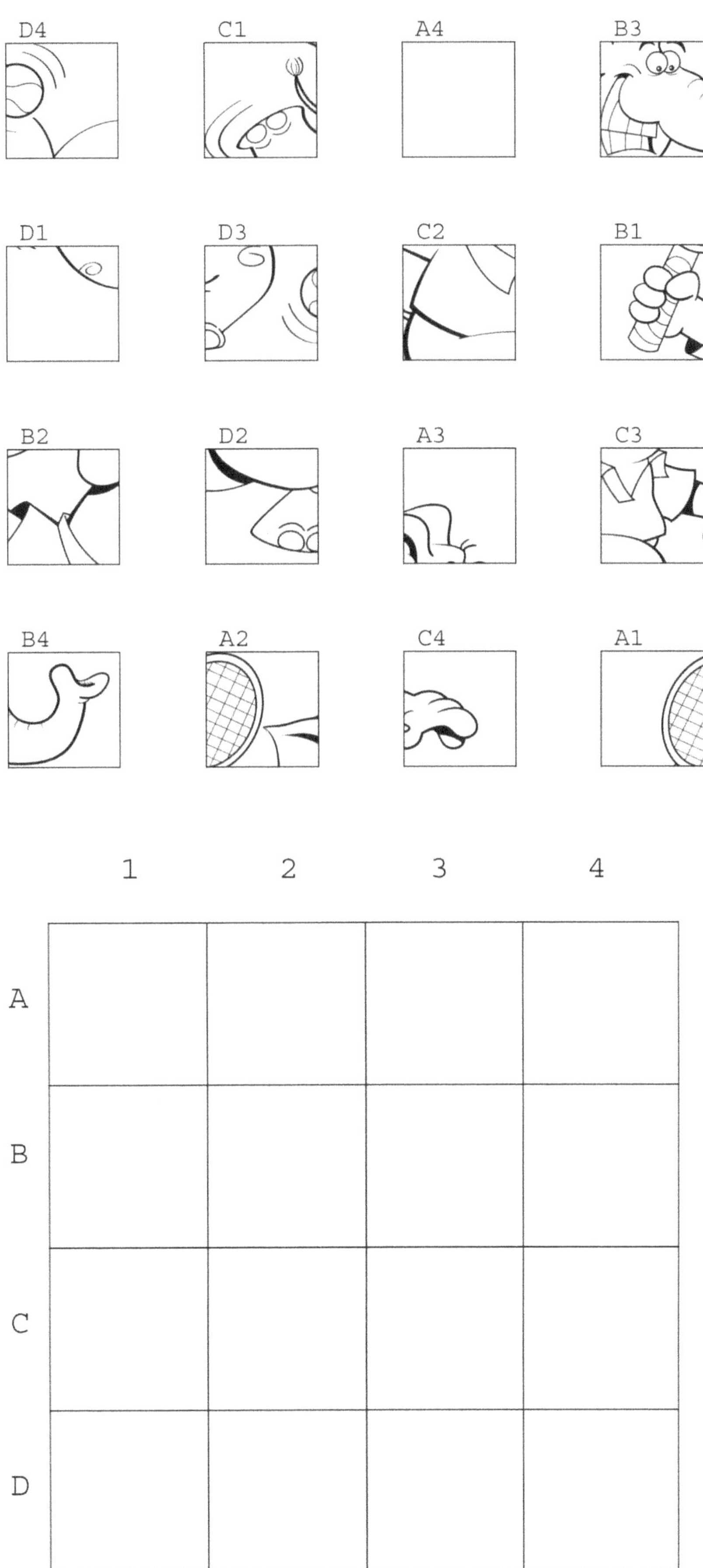

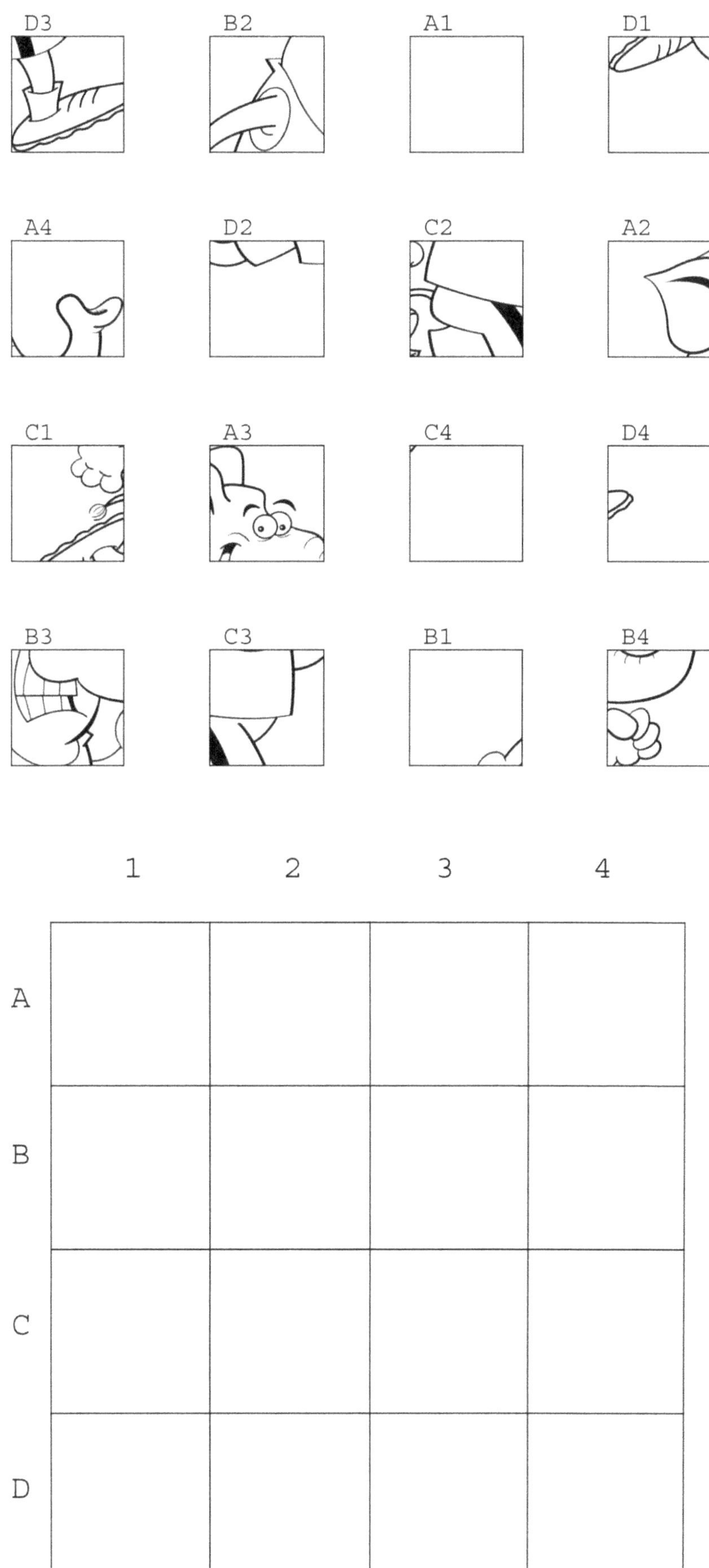

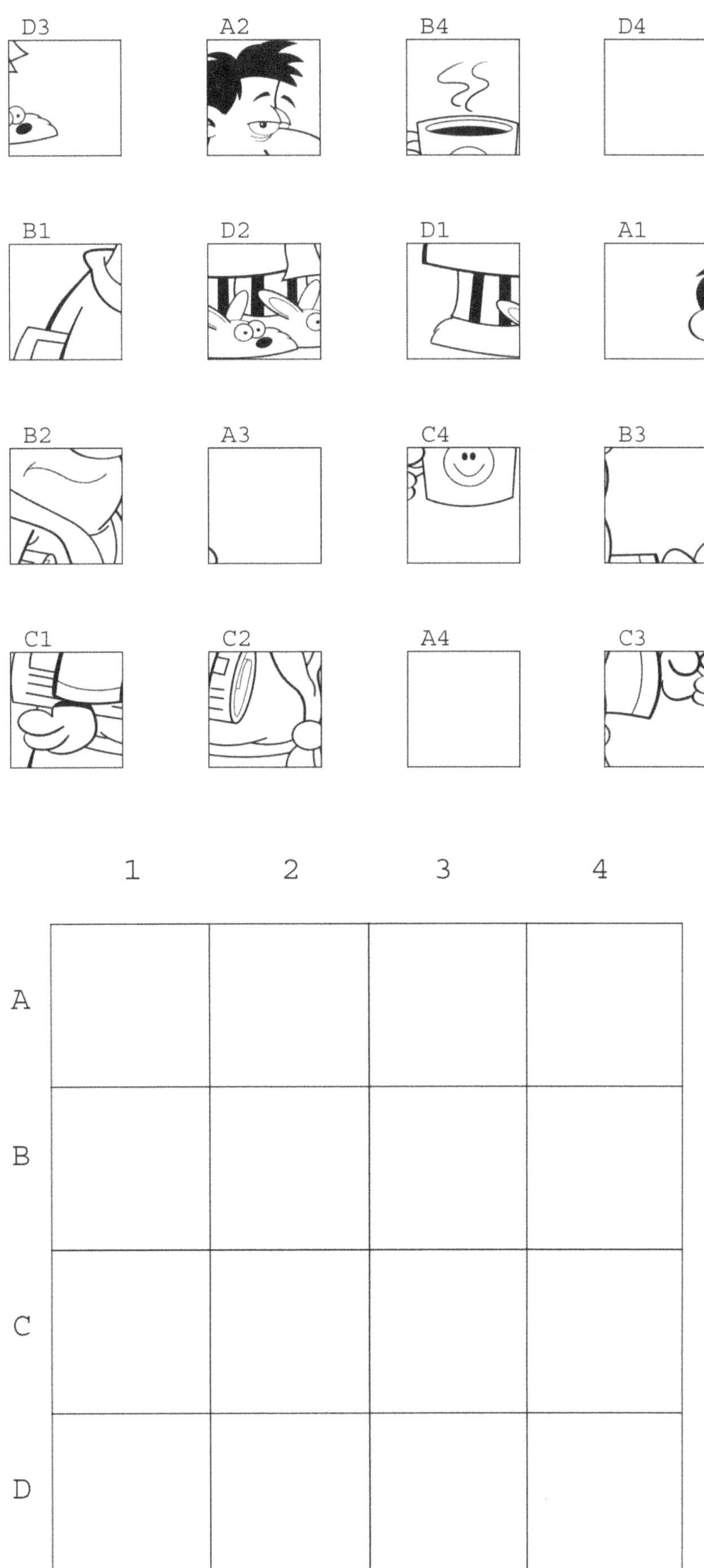

Thank you for completing our book! We appreciate your time and hope you enjoyed the experience. If you're up for more creative challenges, check out our other Pik-Jig books. Explore new grids and dive into the joy of artistic discovery. Happy drawing!

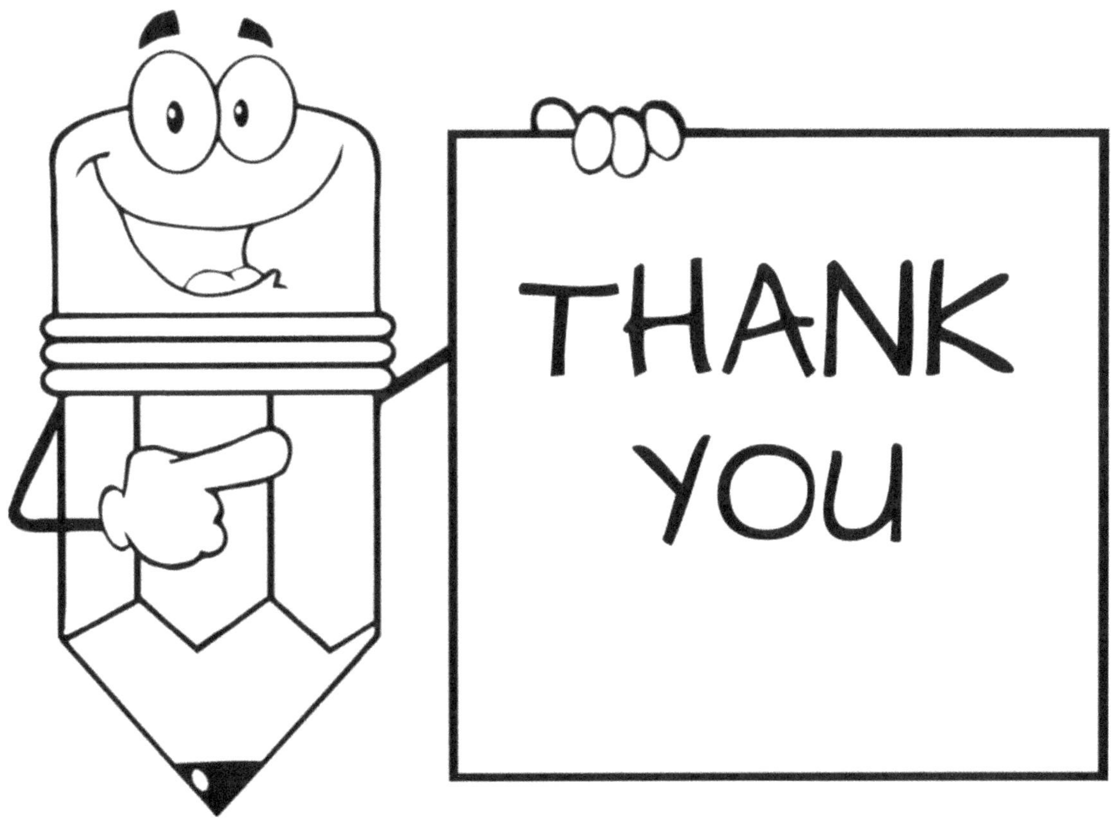